The Date Night Manifesto

A booster shot for relationships

Sophia Ledingham

"... add some spice to date nights while building stronger
relationships." —*Kirkus Reviews*

Cover design and illustration by Kate Forrester

Matador
9 Priory Business Park,
Wistow Road, Kibworth Beauchamp,
Leicestershire. LE8 0RX
Tel: (+44) 116 279 2299
Fax: (+44) 116 279 2277
Email: books@troubador.co.uk
Web: www.troubador.co.uk/matador

ISBN 978 1784621 162

British Library Cataloguing in Publication Data.
A catalogue record for this book is available from the British Library.

Typeset by Troubador Publishing Ltd, Leicester, UK
Printed and bound by CPI Group (UK) Ltd, Croydon, CR0 4YY

Matador is an imprint of Troubador Publishing Ltd

Many years ago my man—who shall be known as "Himself"—asked me to write down what I wanted from my requested Date Night.

At that time I couldn't articulate what I was looking for. But now, after fifteen years of regular Date Nights, I've been able to shape and refine a Manifesto: 16 guiding Principles or Intentions, for a successful Date Night.

Each Principle stems from one or more actual Date experiences. You will see as you read through the Manifesto that I have learnt most from those that *flopped*, failing to yield any romance. Now you can learn and benefit, like Himself and I have, from my mistakes.

It's taken me many years, but here it is.

To Himself,
who is a great date.

Contents

THE INTRODUCTORY BIT

THE INTRODUCTORY BIT

What Is Date Night?

A Date Night is a romantic evening for two people who are in an established relationship.

That's right, a romantic evening. Not just any old "let's pop down to Pizza Hut" evening. Not even a "let's order pizza in and snuggle in front of the TV" evening. A Date Night is a proper date. With your partner.

"But we're committed already," you say. "Why do we need a Date Night?"

Well, think about this.

Maybe you work hard to be the 'host or hostess with the mostess'. You've perfected your party charm and you'd never dream of upsetting your guests. Maybe you pride yourself on finessing your corporate relationships. You make a note to remember the names of your boss's children or a client's wife, or a staff member's holiday plans. And here's the point: just look at the energy you invest in entertaining colleagues, clients and friends. Do you invest the same effort for your 'other half'? Unfortunately most of us don't.

Yet colleagues and clients will come and go, friends hopefully less so. But our significant other, committed life partner, husband or wife is someone you intend to be with for a much longer period; even 'until death do us part'.

Date Night, then, is an evening where you invest energy in nurturing a romantic relationship. *This book is a practical guide to romance.*

How would you describe a romantic evening? Perhaps...

- a candlelit Valentine's dinner with roses and champagne...
- walking hand in hand along a beach into a majestic sunset...
- cuddling on a rug in front of a cosy fireplace.

Maybe you'd recall memorable evenings on holiday, or let your imagination take you to the most romantic of settings...

- a bottle of wine with a view of the Eiffel Tower...
- a horse and carriage ride through New York's Central Park...
- a glamorous dinner at a Balinese beach resort...
- an evening gondola ride in Venice...
- a penthouse suite with city views and an enormous spa bath...
- horse-riding bareback behind a handsome stranger, with hair and white robes a-flowing—OK stop daydreaming right there.

Mills and Boon, the hallmark of the romance novel, is unfortunately not based in reality. Neither are many scenes from television and movies. You may live on the other side of the world from Paris, you may not be able to afford a *Sex and the City* lifestyle or your holidays might be unavoidably child-centred. And while we're on the subject of romantic stereotypes, the reality may be that your 'knight in shining armour' or 'dark, dashing silent type' is prone to a receding hairline and a paunch, and is partial to sports television. Or that your 'English rose' or 'girl next door' is a hazard in the kitchen, a sucker for reality programs, and lets her leg hair grow in winter. *This book helps you get real about romance.*

Getting real about romance means recognising that it is harder now in a committed relationship than it ever was in your early days. Why? Because romance involves a sense of mystery, excitement and remoteness from everyday life. Remember those 'butterflies in the stomach' from your first Dates? The anticipation... will she... won't he? Well that surge of excitement is probably long gone, or has at least lost its lightening strike. As a couple, your patterns of conversation are now entrenched in daily life: "What are we doing this weekend?", "Did you book the car in for a service?" Such dialogue will hardly foster a feeling of romance. *This book helps you take responsibility for the romance in your life.*

To boost romance, you'll need to redirect the conversation away from the usual domestic details. And let's not forget that being romantic requires us to be lovable and loving. Take note—a romantic time for two doesn't necessarily involve sex. There is more importance placed on the emotions of love, intimacy, compassion, and appreciation rather than physical pleasure. But... putting effort into making your spouse or partner feel great could well make him or her feel more partial to a little bedroom action. So whilst a romantic evening may or may not involve physical intimacy, it does involve a loving time, where you feel emotionally connected, special and attractive.

It's easy to take the other for granted, so being romantic, loving and lovable, requires focus. This is where having a Date Night can be especially helpful. But still—why is 'any other evening out' not necessarily a Date Night? Because there isn't always a shared understanding about the romantic intent of the evening. You may go out for convenience, being too tired or uninspired to cook – "let's go down to that little Thai place". On such evenings, it may end up being a wonderful romantic time. However, you're very likely to end up catching up on household administration, talking about the trivialities of the day, sharing frustrations or making future plans. Or, in fact, not talking much at all. All of which is typical couple behaviour.

At this point, a sceptic might say *"Isn't Date Night a bit... contrived?"*

Why yes, it is. It is the contrived nature of Date Night that aims to make it romantic.

The *Oxford Dictionary* definition of 'contrive' is 'to create or bring about (an object or a situation) by deliberate use of skill and artifice'. Let's learn from our early dating years and those first Date experiences, which are in themselves highly orchestrated events. When you first meet someone special you make an effort to have a great time with them. You think carefully about the practicalities of the evening: from what to wear and styling your hair, to the ideal location and how to get there in good time. You might ponder what to share about yourself, and safe yet stimulating topics of conversation. See? Skill and artifice.

Generally we do make a tremendous effort for first Dates. If your dating memory is failing you, which is a sure sign of your established relationship, ask someone who is on (or back on) the dating scene, how much time they invest in preparing and anticipating a Date. It is the forethought, awareness and attention that help to make the night romantic. It is these elements that *contrive* to bring about an ideal outcome! And remember the formality of the first Date invite? One of you invites the other on a Date. You agree on the time and arrangements. Underlining this agreement to the Date is the shared, implicit understanding about the hoped-for romantic intent of the evening.

Let's not underplay the importance of these mutual romantic understandings from the past. After all it was these first Dates which launched the relationship that you have now! But while those were about getting together and increasing your 'being together', you are now very much together. In a live-in relationship, married or otherwise, partners normally make assumptions about the time they spend together. Often the intent of an evening is not spelled out and can lead to miscommunications. For example, Lauren learnt that her husband Frank's "Let me cook you a steak on Friday", wasn't actually an invite for a romantic evening in. He was really communicating "Let me cook you a steak, so that I can then catch the football on television; if we go out, I'll miss the game". In which case there is no romantic intent. Lauren's curve-enhancing little black dress went unnoticed by Frank who was fixated on the game.

So yes, your Date Night *should* be contrived. Contrive away! Because *you* are taking the time to do so, you'll clearly communicate your romantic objective. Then you will both recognise that intimacy is the order of the evening. *This book provides a guide to contriving a successful Date Night experience.*

Welcome to the journey! By the time you finish the final page of this book, you will be armed with simple, practical techniques for many a great Date Night. You'll be injecting some sparkle back into your usual routine, *and* making a regular investment in the future of your relationship!

Is This Right for Us?

All kinds of couples love the enriched connection that comes from Date Night. You'll be surprised! Are you child-free, or do you have one, two or more adorable mini-mes? Are you in your first serious committed relationship, third-time lucky, or heading for your golden anniversary? Be it two or forty-two years together, there's a lot to discover from Date Night. Once the cloak of daily domesticity disappears, you'll find yourself revealing your romantic and attentive self, perhaps even channelling your inner Romeo. You'll feel special and will be connecting with your other half in an intimate and meaningful way. Using the Date Night Manifesto guarantees that you'll discover new things about each other… even if you've been together for what feels like a life-time.

Whether you're a proven romantic maestro, affection-shy, or just plain out of practice, using the Date Night Manifesto will put the big 'R' back in your relationship. Romance! So whatever your situation: newly living together, career focused professionals, dedicated to parenting or maturing empty nesters—this book is for you.

Newly Living Together

Recently married? Or just moved in together, to 'live in sin'? Regardless of your status, new couples really can benefit from introducing a regular Date Night early on in the relationship, when patterns of behaviour are being moulded; before they become established and that little bit harder to change.

For you, romance and passion are still the main feature. The butterflies in your stomach, markings of that initial chemistry, may still flutter their tiny wings. However, you may be finding that you need to work *harder* to keep the magic alive. Your time together has changed! It's no longer purely focused on the romantic, your desire for each other, and your wishes and dreams for the future. You need a Date Night to overcome the romantic hazards on the road ahead.

Once you are living together, you are no longer the absolute centre of each other's attention. Before cohabiting, you needed to *plan* to spend time together, and that time was enjoyably, mutually focused on each other. In fact you couldn't keep your hands off each other, right? Now that you're under the same roof being all domestic, your mate may choose to consume hours surfing the internet, watching television, on the phone or working on a hobby, rather than spending spare time concentrating on you. Before you lived together, this transaction of 'you' time versus 'me' time was less apparent. And what's more, someone has to take out the garbage. This new together-every-day time isn't the romantic picture you painted in your mind, but is punctuated with dull household tasks and tiresome decision-making. Even if those seem exciting at first due to the newness of your shared household, believe me—they soon become commonplace.

Living together means that you are now having to agree on all kinds of domestic arrangements. Is it OK to leave loo seat up? How often should we chuck the bed linen in the wash? Who pays the bills? Should we be saving money on the satellite TV or splashing out on organic vegetables? Some agreements will come easily; others could become a bone of contention. Without the benefit of a long history together, you don't necessarily know where the arguments will lie, so you may be naively walking into them. Take picture-perfect couple Rachel and Jake—she a stylist and he a professional athlete. They'd just celebrated moving into a swanky central city neighbourhood, yet the ink had barely dried on their first joint tenancy when they were found quarrelling over who left the lid off the milk. Then there was the public row at the chic deli over the benefits of margarine versus butter. Hydrogenated fats may be not beneficial to one's health, but the arguments weren't beneficial to the health of Rachel and Jake's relationship—they didn't make it to the end of the rental term. Mercifully still together, Himself and I spent days debating over the merit of a 'shoes off at the front door' policy, and—worse still—disagreeing about the display of framed certificates on the walls. You just can't predict some of these disputes, yet when they occur, they can easily extinguish the romantic flame.

You are still learning about each other, but you're less able to control what your partner sees and hears. They are now privy to what's behind your immaculate presentation to the outside world; your morning face, your hair in its natural state, your second-best and third-best underwear, and the ungainly way you like to sprawl across the couch after a long hard day, while eating takeaways off a newspaper on the floor.

Meanwhile, you are becoming all too aware of their habits. They may cut their toenails without regard to where the clippings fly; they may like to take the laptop to bed for some late night social networking; they may undress by dropping their jeans and underpants in one go then stepping out of them, leaving denim 'cowpats' on the floor. Got an ensuite bathroom? Then you're both going to hear each other eliminating bodily wastes. Yes kids, the cloak of mystery is rapidly disappearing.

So don't be naïve! Even for the most hand-holding, eye-gazing, baby-talking couples, living together forces familiarity and introduces romance-foiling domestic hazards. But observing the Date Night Manifesto can set you up for many years of romance, helping you to preserve the essential elements of your attraction and commitment to each other. Start early—start *now*—and you have the opportunity to be truly great at Date Nights. Like any form of activity the more you do it, the better you'll get.

Busy Professionals: Career Rich, Romance Poor

Whether you are married or not, would you want to be wedded to your work? Does your commitment to your job, company or career mean that your work often takes priority over your partner and relationship?

Himself once suggested that my work was the 'third person' in our relationship—and this was no love triangle. It was true though; in those early years, I was guilty often of putting business needs before relationship needs. I even shortened a ten day holiday, because of the prospect of winning a lucrative contract for the company I served so ambitiously. As it happened, I didn't win the new business and have since learnt not to waste hard-earned vacation days. I also confess that it took a couple of years of his encouragement before I agreed to take an *entire day off* during a seven day week. In my mind, I would justify the endless toil because "the business needed me". I didn't realise that the relationship also needed me.

Conducting an ongoing 'affair' with work wasn't exclusive to me however, with Himself also prone to workaholism. "I'm not top of your priority list!" you'd hear me vent. First came his work, next came his gym, and *then* me—on a good week. Whatever the case, if you don't feel like a priority, you don't feel valued or special. You just feel taken for granted. It's not fun.

When you've been in a relationship for a number of years, you've ironed out the creases of the domestic arrangements and you're able to successfully predict much of your partner's behaviour. Yet, lodged safely in this comfort zone, you are at most risk of taking the relationship as a given. My colleague Rodney, returning from one of his many business trips, found that his wife of twenty-five years had left him. Rodney was beyond devastation; they had only just celebrated their silver wedding anniversary. Whilst he was working hard to navigate company politics, embed a new team and finesse his global corporate relationships, Rodney wasn't giving sufficient energy to his most important relationship. Colleagues and clients will come and go, but our significant other, our committed life partner, husband or wife is someone we are intending to be with for a much longer period. A lifelong period. Maybe relationship insurance should be added to our employment contracts! After all, these cover hours of work, holidays, pension arrangements, medical and life insurance—let's see a clause that states 'this job could endanger your relationship health'. The reality is that work can often consume your focus, whether at the office or not. Now by no means am I suggesting that you *don't* work hard, pursue a fulfilling career or show your commitment to your employer. What I am very strongly suggesting is this: be mindful of your relationship's vulnerability, respect your time together, and actively pursue real opportunities for romance.

If 'time is the new money', creating more time with an increasingly busy work life can be as much a challenge as making more money. The value is different yet equally vital. Finding time for a regular Date Night represents a meaningful investment in your relationship and your long-term prosperity as partners. Money analogies—don't you love them!

Parents: Children Rich but Romance Poor

Kids. Those loveable little user-uppers of much time and energy.

It has been controversially noted that parents often report statistically *lower* levels of happiness and marital satisfaction, compared with non-parents.[1] Don't get me wrong, parenthood is littered with absolute joy. Baby's first smile, first steps, first performance in a school play, birthdays and family occasions, simply the satisfaction of breeding itself, especially when meeting wider family expectations. However, these parental pleasures are usually experienced momentarily and do not always translate to day-to-day happiness. The hard work of parenting means that domestic life is overwhelmed by thankless tasks such as toilet training, coordinating the school run, overseeing homework, and trying to contain the incessant mountains of laundry.

Obviously, you now have way *less* time and energy for yourselves. Despite the pending arrival of a babysitter, Penny—who has three children under the age of six—tells me that the mere thought of getting spruced up for a night out sounds like a chore rather than a treat! I hear from Penny how hard it is to put on a nice pair of tights while a toddler is clinging to your leg, or to wield a hair straightener while firmly advising a five-year-old of the disciplinary result of pelting his little sister with matchbox cars. How can you put on a sensuous perfume when a full nappy demands your attention? And to initiate a Date Night on top of all this? Are you kidding?

You *know* the perpetual presence of the children is a passion killer. They are not houseguests who are going to leave on Sunday. They are always there, and they don't respect your privacy. Even the most intimate bedroom moments can be interrupted by a small visitor seeking comfort from a bad dream. Good heavens, you can barely even relax while seated on the loo! (Penny will attest to this.) They might go to school, play sport or go on a 'play date', but their complete dependence on you is ever present. For new parents, getting to bed *later* than ten in the evening is a thing of the past, now that little Max or Maxine is up with the lark at five. And as for teenagers, needing to be on your guard for youthful antics might compete for your attention on a Date Night.

With this in mind, you probably have less enthusiasm or opportunity for intimacy than before the sprogs arrived on the scene. Some of my friends tell me they are just too tired to think of their partner, let alone be romantic. That any spare time is coveted and justifiably translates to 'me' time rather than 'we' time. I often hear couples negotiating 'me' time: "If you look after the kids on Saturday whilst I play golf, then I'll skip my Tuesday evening bike ride and come straight home so you can make it to pottery class". Between attending to the children and guarding any 'me' time, it's no wonder 'we' time is in short supply. When you do get together, book the babysitter and manage a night out, you probably find the evening consumed with domestic discussions, family arrangements and household administration. That's if you don't fall asleep at the restaurant table and face-plant into your soup.

Where's the potential for romance in this? Should we blindly assume that shared parenting *compensates* for a loss in shared romance? A working mother said to me that she feels compelled to spend any free energy focused on entertaining her children rather than her spouse. It is admirable to be so devoted to your children yet it is not without risk—her pre-schoolers are not about to walk out on her, yet her husband might.

Similarly, there are some parents who appear to be more 'in love' with their kids than their partner. Speaking with one doting father, who was explaining to me how he has no time to take his wife out on a Date, yet in the next sentence he's proudly telling me how he's socialising his four-year-old to be restaurant savvy by taking him for outings to cafes. Sounds like the child is the one now benefiting from Dates!

Top US bloke-blogger Brenton Balvin, an advocate of Date Nights, says there are all kinds of reasons parents give for not having a Date

Night; no time, no money, and no babysitter being amongst the most popular excuses. Brenton asks, "If your spouse confessed to having an affair, would you concede it was OK because, after all, you never dated each other after the wedding day—because you didn't have the time, the money, or a babysitter for the kids?"

In days gone by, the parental role and family duty was a totally valid excuse for not nurturing romance. Those were the days when couples would stay together for the children and possibly out of respect for their church and marital vows. For some, the shame of divorce was more fearful than persisting in a loveless union.

But these days of course, we are more individualistic and self-serving, and more demanding about fulfilling our relationship needs than ever before. A lack of romance by either party can easily lead to a broken partnership, be it marriage or otherwise. Using the Date Night Manifesto will reinforce the romance in the relationship. It will focus you on the positive, on each other, having fun and crucially putting aside—if just for a few hours—the distractions of parenting, household needs and decision making.

It's worth noting that Barack Obama managed to take time out to whisk wife Michelle away for a Date Night. He jetted her to New York for dinner and a Broadway show. If one of the busiest family-men in the world can make time for a Date... so can you.

Empty Nesters and Retirees: Rediscovering the big R

You are likely to be in your fifties, sixties or seventies, with the benefit of a mature relationship. Wow. As a couple, you've weathered life's storms, from family fall-outs to health and money concerns. You have a valuable connection, a shared history, that bonds you together. But do you still have romance?

Many long-term couples have spent the majority of their years together dedicated to their roles as parents or as professionals. Anniversaries, Valentine's Day, birthdays – these may have been times for intimacy and displays of affection. But why hide it away until special occasions? Now that you are retired, or your children have left home, you can refocus on your relationship, and by introducing a regular Date Night, rekindle a deeper level of romance.

When I'm on vacation I've been surprised to discover the number of couples who are holidaying without their children for the *first time* in fifteen or twenty years. Oh boy! I'm amazed that relationships can survive for so long without so much as a romantic weekend away. For these couples, their role as parents usually took priority over any rapidly fading romantic wishes. And then, after years of distraction, prioritising the romantic connection can be quite daunting.

Lilith was delighted about the prospect of a weekend away with her husband—just the two of them. She could not remember the last time they were away without friends or an assortment of their six children. Now here they were—all children grown up and gone from the nest. On realising the rare nature of the weekend, she then became so worried about what they would talk about, and what they would do, that she called friends for advice. Would you believe that she smuggled tiny conversation cue cards into her weekend bag. Barry was surprised to find Lilith wearing her reading glasses all weekend!

Lilith may well be worried. She'd probably heard about the growing trend for relationships to break up after children have flown the coop, or during retirement. In many cases, the relationship had broken down much earlier but the couple stayed together for the sake of the children. In other situations, family and work distracted the couple from realising that something was amiss. Fellow book club member Martha, confided that it wasn't until her sons left home that she was confronted with the stark reality of being 'Fred's wife'. Fred required her to be at his golf club each weekend, to socialise in a certain way, with a certain crowd and even to look a certain way. Mild-mannered Martha shocked her world, including her children, by leaving her husband. She is now remarried, has let her hair down, and says that she's enjoying being truer to herself. Free from Fred, she's actually found that she quite likes golf! Today people in their fifties, sixties and seventies are healthier than ever and are less likely to stay in a loveless relationship, when they have numerous opportunities to fulfil their personal goals and desires. Just because you have had twenty or thirty years together doesn't guarantee forty or fifty.

Like children leaving home, retirement can be a welcomed stage, but—what's this? Why doesn't it seem like the extended holiday you hoped for? Initially, many people find it unsettling without the comfort of their regular schedule. The self-esteem can take a battering without the reassurance of that tried and tested work identity. No longer the CEO or the go-to staff member, now you are kicking around the house at a loose end. *Or* you might deal with change easily and see retirement as an opportunity to explore your hidden talents as an artist, furniture restorer, charity fundraiser, or active member at the tennis club. Whatever your personal situation and goals, you will find retirement introducing changes into your relationship: a different attitude, a wider or narrower circle of friends, even fresh responsibilities. The most obvious shift in relationship terms is that you have the prospect of an extra ten, twenty or forty hours per week together. Reality check— how keen *are you* to be together? Will spending more 'we' time feel like a chore? Will it be uplifting? What on earth will you talk about? After all this time, you're forced to reflect on the nature and quality of your relationship. Choices include how to avoid each other, how to avoid conflict, or how to invest in your relationship and put some effort into taking it to a higher level. It's your call. And if you choose the latter, following this Manifesto will certainly help.

Yes, retirement, or the newly empty nest, can be the catalyst for renewed romantic purpose.

The Date Night Manifesto will offer you a framework for resetting your romantic barometer. It will take you out of your romantic rut. And note too—it will take you out of your comfort zone. But nothing ventured, nothing gained, right? Wouldn't you, with a little effort, enjoy renewed interest, rekindled romance, re-established closeness and intimacy? Wouldn't you like to feel special and share desires for your future together? Now it's just the two of you, you can really take advantage of new-found time, space or money in pocket to invest in planning for your Date Nights.

Whether you have clocked up double-digit anniversaries or still savouring the wedding cake, the Manifesto's 16 Principles will give you more to celebrate. Before I share them with you, I'll reveal the conscience-stricken state that drove me to discover them.

The Birth of
the Date Night Manifesto

It was a miserable afternoon in Ireland. The wind was up and the rain came down, reflecting my mood perfectly. I even wore black from top to toe. The previous night's much anticipated romantic evening with Himself had begun and ended disastrously. And I knew it was largely my doing. A girlfriend joined me for a sympathetic afternoon glass of wine and asked me 'why the long face', and 'why do you feel so responsible?'

Why was it my fault? Let me count the *ways*. I'd turned up late, I was in a sulk because of my day, the weather, and the ladder in my expensive new tights. I'd bitched about the service, moaned about the quantity of sauce on my porterhouse, berated Himself for his choice of tie, shot down his attempts to lighten the atmosphere, and done nothing to quell the bad feeling that started to rise between us. Before I knew it, I had given my intrepid listener a lengthy list of what NOT to do on a Date.

And suddenly, after years of Date Nights with Himself and painfully trying to define the makings of a good Date, I had a 'eureka' moment. I felt liberated! Let there be no more uncertainty about the fate of my Date Night! Let the success of Date Night *no longer* be dependant on our mood, the state of the nation, the quality of the restaurant, the seductiveness of the lighting and decor, the customer service, the ease of the journey, or the texture of the restroom's toilet paper.

> The Date Night needed me to be diligent and pro-active.
> The Date Night needed me to take responsibility for creating *success,* not failure.
> The Date Night needed… no, not rules… Intentions. It needed a set of guiding Principles.

I realised romance was in *my* hands. My girlfriend had never seen such a transformation, as I hugged her and rushed home, beaming, to start writing down these Principles. The Date Night Manifesto was born!

The 16 Principles of the Date Night Manifesto took shape as I listened to other stories of romantically challenged evenings. It seems we all expect romance will find its way into an occasion, then are disappointed when it doesn't. And yes, it is our fault.

For example, early one morning there was a knock at my door. It was my Swedish neighbour Agatha, a fitness instructor in her early thirties, married to a lawyer for three years. Agatha looked agitated. Had she missed one of her self-imposed pre-dawn workouts? No. She had spent the night sleeping in the spare room. She claimed her marriage now lacked any romance and her desire for her husband was close to zero. So we sat down with a cup of coffee and gazed out across the garden to contemplate this unspeakable thing she'd just spoken: no desire for her husband! This wasn't what marriage was supposed to be about. Not in this day and age.

Did you know romance is only *recently* associated with marriage? I know—shocking isn't it. As long as there have been relationships and passion, surely there have been romantic evenings? Yet it's unlikely that such evenings, or romance *at all,* appeared on the agenda for our wedded ancestors. Throughout much of human history, it was thought that a marriage based on romance was foolish, a selfish pursuit of one's own happiness and inevitably headed for disaster. No, marriage had more practical considerations to serve! Such as establishing political connections, especially in royal or noble circles; preserving wealth if you were lucky enough to be born into it, and marrying into it if you weren't; sustaining religious expectations, and of course the all-important begetting of the family heir. These unions were normally arranged. Until the mid-twentieth century in western societies, parents had a large influence in selecting an appropriate spouse.

But back to Agatha. I asked her for the specifics of how she and her husband spent their time together, and she talked me through a number of evenings. To me, these sounded highly administrative. The couple had been focused for several months on trying to purchase property and it consumed all their down-time together. An evening was typically spent huddled around an Excel spreadsheet, discussing budgets, cash flow and timelines. Their tight finances meant that an evening out was rare, but even then they'd end up talking about how they could save money. How can you feel sexy over spreadsheets? It's no wonder desire had been forced into the back seat. Sure, a married couple needs a place to live. But romance needs to be kept alive, so that it too can occupy a new home.

Mary, a physician, has instigated a weekly Date Night for her and her partner of twelve years. Mary is proud that she is focusing more on the relationship which has spawned two children under five years old. Yet here's the reality of her Date Night: a regular movie night, in which the couple have little opportunity to talk to each other. Go figure! I enquired further and learnt that her partner chooses the movies, normally action, thrillers or sci-fi—all the things *he* likes to watch. What, not even a romantic comedy? Does Mary care? No, because her Date Night offers her two hours off from looking after the kids.

You know what I'm about to say. This weekly outing isn't a Date Night, but a well-earned, child-free evening—an occasion that some parents can only dream of. Did I enquire about the resulting romance? No. It seemed so terribly unlikely.

Edith is a leading figure in a regional women's network. Possessed with a bubbly personality, she has a talent for arousing the enthusiasm of all around her and getting a party underway. Edith has been married to a prominent professor for thirty-five years; small, thin and shy in company, he relies on Edith as the sociable face of their partnership.

I bumped into Edith at Starbucks, and unusually for this upbeat lady, she was moaning about a restaurant she and her husband had recently dined at. It was empty, the service was slow; it was, she felt, unjustifiably expensive. "How could anyone like that place?" she wondered.

It turns out this particular dinner was a Date Night with her husband. "Did you share these thoughts with him?" I asked. "Yes, of course." "Did you have a romantic evening?" "No." Well, better luck next time.

Whether or not the restaurant was at fault, Edith had found too much to complain about. And this—the complaining—was the nail in the coffin of that evening's romance.

These stories represent just a few of the many reasons that this Manifesto has come about. But take heart. I've found the solution to achieving a romantic evening with my partner. And you'll find it on the very next page.

Date Night Manifesto

Part One: Date Night Prep

1. Get Your Beauty Sleep
2. Book Your Table for Two
3. Find Your Date Night Finery
4. Arrive 'in Smile'
5. Romance Won't Wait (Don't Be Late)

Part Two: Date Night Decorum

6. Hang off Their Every Word
7. Every Venue Has a Silver Lining
8. Toast Your Togetherness
9. The Etiquette of Flattery
10. Reveal More (but No Strip Tease—Yet)
11. Wanted: Good Sense of Humour

Part Three: Date Night Vitamins

12. Negativity No-Nos
13. Be a Lover Not a Fighter
14. Keep Your Eyes on the Prize (Your Beloved)
15. Take a Break from 'Decisions We Must Make'
16. Shelve Those Domestic Details

The 16 Principles

The Manifesto's 16 Principles are divided into three parts: Date Night Prep; Date Night Decorum; and Date Night Vitamins. The Date Night Prep Principles work together to set the stage for romance, with five Intentions that you'll perform before the Date itself. The Principles in parts two and three guide your on-Date behaviours. Date Night Decorum is all about your on-Date etiquette and Date Night Vitamins are vital for promoting dating health. You will see that these on-Date Principles are focused on talking: from what to say and how best to say it, to what you should avoid during your Date.

However, remember this! The Manifesto's Principles are not rules, but *Intentions*. You needn't abide by *all* to achieve success. If you deviate, I'm not going to magically appear and slap you on the wrist! These Intentions are designed to help you. They're based on common sense and practical experience, combined with psychological theory and scientific evidence. Each represents a building block towards a successful Date. Not all Intentions are created equal—there are two underpinning Principles, which are fundamental to the success of the evening. These are Principle 6 – *Hang off Their Every Word* and Principle 12 – *Negativity No-Nos*. Believe me, both of these are vital 'secret attendants' on your Date. Without them along for the ride, I doubt you'll be discovering much in the way of romance!

Each Principle has its own chapter, in which I explain its significance. Your understanding will be aided by not only theory explained, but actual experiences from couples to further elaborate on my own dating knowledge. Each chapter ends practically, with clear action points to prepare you for dating action.

Yes, you will find some Intentions more comfortable than others. But I challenge you to explore fresh territory and have a good go at those less-developed Intentions. The pay-off will be learning more about each other, and being able to connect on a deeper level. To help self-awareness of your dating performance, there is a scoring sheet on page 201. It may seem like an enormous feat to fully operate all 16 Principles to the highest level, but through staying aware and keeping up your practice, you *can* develop your dating skills in order to confidently ignite the romantic flame in your relationship. Then, no matter how well you have scored on the page, you have scored in your affair of the heart.

Putting Your Best Foot Forward

Are you eager to get your Date Night Manifesto started? You might be already engaged in regular Date Nights—lucky you! The Manifesto will encourage an upgrade in your Dates. If you are not already on the Date Night wagon, you may need to introduce the idea of Date Nights to your partner. So follow the Manifesto—it outlines the best practice from the start.

In this chapter, you'll find all the mechanics of *Putting Your Best Foot Forward*, including which Principles to start with, and who might be best at organising the Date.

But let's say your other half is not as willing to give the Date Night Manifesto a shot. You're not going to let that stop you, are you? Are you! See *Dealing with 'Date Night Resistance'* on page 203 for strategies to win over even the most stubborn partner or spouse.

Already conducting regular Date Nights? You may have found, like Himself and I, that some have been great, even a little romantic, while others dissolve into domestic discussions. "We stare blankly at each other in restaurants... then I start making to-do lists," confessed *Sunday Times* journalist Shane Watson about her Date Nights. Sound familiar? If you haven't embarked on any form of Date Night yet, then 'to-do lists' are your first 'what not to do'. And there's more to come. With the Date Night Manifesto on hand, you have no excuse for poor Date Night etiquette! The Manifesto helps you stay on track, leading to a more intimate and enjoyable evening.

So how do you get started? Obviously it's important that you introduce your mate to the Principles which you are soon to learn about. S/he doesn't need to read this book, though it would be great if they did; you can simply share with them the one page Date Night Manifesto (page 23) or the Date Night score sheet (page 201) both detail the Principles. As the key elements to the evening, the 16 Principles are fairly self explanatory and can be easily interpreted with a little common sense.

I remember one husband being sent the 16 Principles as part of an invitation. In Sandra and Mitch's twelve year marriage, Mitch has always been Mr Romance. However, they'd never set aside actual Date Nights. When Sandra and I were discussing the prospect of a Date Night, she was confident that Mitch would be up for it. Sandra decided to set the first Date Night on Mitch's birthday evening by securing a table at a popular, sought-after restaurant and sending him a formal invite to the evening with the one page Date Night Manifesto also enclosed. This couple regularly attend black-tie functions and other formal events, so Mitch was well versed with this style of invite. But instead of travel directions, or a program for the evening, his inclusion was the Date Night Manifesto's 16 Principles. This really appealed to Mr Romance— their Date Nights were off to a good start.

Whether you make an elaborate gesture of sharing the Date Night Manifesto, or simply discuss it over coffee at the kitchen table, you'll need to agree which of the 16 Principles to focus on first. It can be a bit daunting to attempt all from the start, and we don't want your partner to run screaming from the idea. Remember these Principles are *Intentions,* not rules, so no one should expect ruthless vigilance.

Want to take baby steps? I recommend beginning with the following:

Principle 6 – *Hang off Their Every Word* – being attentive
Principle 12 – *Negativity No-Nos* – avoiding negativity
Principle 16 – *Shelve Those Domestic Details* – discard your 'to-do' list.

Focusing on these three Principles will find you concentrating on each other, actively listening and engaging in positive and meaningful conversation, and avoiding the romance-fizzler of domestic issues. In this way, you are matching much of the Date etiquette from your early dating years and perhaps that first date passion! To heighten sensuality, add in:

Principle 2 – *Book Your Table for Two* – your romantic setting
Principle 3 – *Find Your Date Night Finery* – dressing to impress.

Yes! You're underway.

Alternatively you and your partner may choose a different set of Intentions. You could kick-start the Date Night Manifesto with your strengths—behaviours that come easily for you. If you're fun loving and good at giving compliments, start with Principle 9 – *The Etiquette of Flattery* and highlight your playfulness with Principle 11 – *Wanted: Good Sense of Humour*. For others, your best behaviour may include the conflict-avoidance of Principle 13 – *Be a Lover Not a Fighter*. Spend a few Dates feeling successful with comfortable Intentions, and you'll think, "hey, this Manifesto lark is not too bad!" With this increased confidence, you'll be more inclined to take on more challenging Intentions.

Some Principles may be more difficult because they're outside your comfort zone. Tackling these first can help if you're after quicker results, as those trickier areas will need a more concentrated effort. There is some logic to this approach: you probably subconsciously employ your strength areas when it comes to romantic opportunities, so you may not see a big difference in intimate connection on Date Night. However, if you focus on addressing a single problem or challenge, you might get a more impressive and immediate response. For example, the person who tends to bring up domestic issues during rare couple time may be surprised at the romantic difference made by setting them aside for another day.

You and your mate may decide to jump in and attempt all 16 Principles. If so, don't freak out if you're not initially great at all of them, and do resist pointing out your partner's (and your own) Manifesto misdemeanours during the Date Night itself—this is a *Negativity No-No*. (See this Principle on page 133). In the days after, you may like to use the score sheet on page 201 to review your Date Night and help clarify areas for improvement. It will take practice to be accomplished in many of the areas. The good news is that Date Night is a regular investment in your relationship, so you should have many years to practise and finetune your dating art.

OK! Now you've agreed to your Intentions, who should initiate and plan the Date? Some couples successfully alternate Date Night organisation, others plan their Dates together, discussing options and preferences from one week to the next. I must confess the organisation proved a sticking point for us, me being of the firm belief that we should *alternate* the role of Date Night organiser. In hindsight however, I was setting up Himself to fail in this role. He wasn't nearly as passionate about keeping current with what was on, new restaurants or key sporting events and concerts. I invariably felt disappointed at his lack of research, which I interpreted as a lack of *thoughtfulness*. Happily, in recent years we have recognised each other's strengths. I now contentedly organise most of our Dates, and Himself expresses thanks and gratitude (Principle 9 — *The Etiquette of Flattery*) for my doing it!

Think carefully about who takes responsibility for Date organisation. Is one of you definitely more organised, or an 'ideas' person, or likes to read your city's going-out guides and websites? You could conduct a few trials until you settle on a method that works for you as a couple.

With the Date Night organiser agreed, at least for the first Date, then you're ready to roll. Where should you go first? Start planning for the Date with the *Date Night Prep* Principles coming next in Part One. If you're one of those people who likes to read endings first, feel free to go straight to the *Date Idea-Sparkers* on page 179.

So *Put Your Best Foot Forward* and get started today. You will be surprised at how good your Date Night can be!

PART ONE:
DATE NIGHT PREP

PART ONE

DATE NIGHT PREP

1. Get Your Beauty Sleep

"Energy creates Energy. It is by spending oneself that one becomes rich."
— Sarah Bernhardt

Lesson from your early dates: Excited by the mystery of a first Date, you arrived energised and ready for action.

A Date Night relaxing? You can get that idea out of your head right now! The outcome may be relaxing, but during the evening you will need to be fully focused and fully engaged. This is *not* an evening to zone out, nod off or make aimless conversation. So the key here is making sure you arrive fully charged and raring to go.

Energy is needed to channel your charming self—and stay on romantic form, restraining those slip-ups that could derail your Date. Academic psychologists now have evidence that shows that when energy is low, self-control is weakened. Not surprisingly, couples tend to treat each other in less desirable ways when their self-control resources are depleted[2]. Getting your beauty sleep will remedy those dark patches under your eyes and fuel your intimacy-focused frame of mind.

To set the tone for romance, start by scheduling the evening for when you are likely to have gained that all important beauty sleep, or are sure you'll be energised. This is an easy Principle—it's simply about choosing the right day. Even if the 'perfect' night or day is hard to come by, certainly some are going to be better for you than others. And obviously don't go scheduling a Date for just after you've run a half marathon, or your partner has just sat a rather difficult exam (and has pulled some all-nighters studying!).

Select the day of your Date carefully, as you would for any other vital social event. Just as you might if you were planning cocktails with pals, a rare evening with your best friend, or hosting a dinner party, you want to be considering any commitments before and after. And you'd prepare, hopefully, to have maximum vitality for the event (and I don't suggest merely dosing up on caffeine!).

Remember when you were on the single scene? Friday or Saturday night Dates were sought after, being the prime dating nights of the week. An invite for a Tuesday night Date could signal a lower level of romantic interest and raise eyebrows as to who your date was seeing at the weekend. But that was then and this is now… and you *will* be seeing your mate this weekend. So you can happily tailor your Dates for any night of the week to capitalise on your flexibility and energy patterns.

When are you Fully Charged?

For starters, what are energy levels like during the week for both of you? Is a Friday more uplifting than a Thursday night, or is a Monday night best because of less work pressure? Are there some no-go days?

For theatre teacher Frederica and consultant Roger, married twenty-eight years, a Saturday night works best. Roger is a self-acknowledged introvert and is often exhausted by a week in a hectic open-plan office, so he likes to recover with a quiet night in, watching the history channel, pottering in his garden shed, or building his model boat. As Frederica explains, it's difficult to get a grunt from him on a Friday, so there's no hope in expecting him to perform for a Date Night. However, by Saturday, I hear, Roger is fully recharged; he's animated and ready for action. That's when theatre-loving Frederica knows she has her romantic co-star.

For me, Fridays are revitalising, upbeat and ideal. A Friday evening affects my mood positively—I welcome the weekend and temporarily let go of work expectations. There'll be no nasty alarm clock blaring at me the next day so I'm at liberty to let my hair down, have a little wine and not worry about the time.

Mondays also work for Himself and I. There is something indulgent about a Monday night Date and it certainly makes for a happier day in the office and start to the week, knowing that you're not going home to do laundry or pay bills, but out! To be romanced!

The good thing about midweek Dates is the restaurant specials, theatre discounts and other deals. The downside is that you're likely to be under more work pressure. Sure, some people can switch off easily when they leave the office, but for others, it's a challenge to leave work at the office door. Take Himself, for example. We tried a Thursday night Date recently and while it wasn't a bad Date, Himself wasn't as relaxed as usual, with a key piece of work to be delivered the next day. Postponing this Date would have been much more successful. This is where it pays to communicate and be sensitive to each other's commitments. Oh—and here's where you reap the advantages of being in an *established* relationship and not on the single dating scene, where you have far less idea about your date's day-to-day life. Using your insider knowledge, you can predict energy levels and sense the scope for romance.

At one time, Himself and I had a regular Monday night Date at a local bar-restaurant. Monday night worked well—not only was it less likely to clash with any work obligations, but we also benefited from a cocktail happy hour. Needless to say, these cocktails helped to bring about good spirits (see Principle 4 – *Arrive 'in Smile'*) regardless of how our day had been.

Consider whether a regular Date Night might work well; for example a recurring Friday night Date or the third Thursday of the month. Then there's no fuss negotiating your evening each time. You also benefit by being able to set up practices to ensure a smooth dating operation, such as travel arrangements, work schedules or child care.

Regular is Fine, but 'Standard' Should be Avoided
Do not let your Dates become standard affairs!

What, then, makes a Date standard rather than special? Too much routine can tip the status. The same time and day of the week coupled with the same event and venue can lead to a predictable evening that loses its romantic zeal. The 'same old, same old' denies you the opportunity to explore Date ideas, build anticipation and share the sense of a special evening. Isabel and David, married for fifteen years with three school-aged children, have a regular Date which is based in a very practical fashion on a Friday night—that's when their trusted babysitter, whom the children adore, is available. But the day of the week and babysitter aren't the only matters that are regulated. Isabel and David also have a set activity: a movie at the same cinema followed by a steak dinner at the same restaurant. Borrrring! It may have started as a Date Night with shared romantic intent, but has now morphed into a fully justified yet fully predictable 'break from the kids' night. Where's the romantic spark?! (See Principle 2 – *Book Your Table for Two*, for more on keeping Date Night special.)

Mercifully our Monday nights of cocktail consumption never reached 'standard' status. Despite our happy hour contributions, the owners failed to keep the restaurant afloat, so our cocktail Dates lasted only a short (but sweet) season.

Too Tired to Date your Mate?

Now for some of you, the concept of having any energy for a Date may cause you to break out a sardonic laugh. "Impossible" you may say, "I have children!" Enough said.

I was talking to my friend Peter, a London-based dentist married to business graduate Layla. As father to a pair of pre-schoolers, here is a man who stood firmly by his belief that for parents, there is simply no good time for a Date. He cynically smirked as I discussed capitalising on energy levels, pointing out that getting up twice a night to attend to bad dreams, wet beds and thirst requirements means that he and Layla are perpetually sleep-deprived. Sympathetic to Peter are Jacquie and Don, medical doctors who have their hands full with two-year-old twins. Recognising that two bubs could well mean waving bye-bye to romance, Jacquie and Don committed, as new parents, to making time for Date Night. They tell me that in the first months of parenthood they made a big deal for their first Date Night, securing a table in a fine dining restaurant with a five course gourmet menu. Excitement to be out together, and wearing clothes that weren't stained with baby milk-vomit, was swiftly followed by fatigue. Our duo was seen nodding asleep over the ginger-infused tiramisu. The solution for Jacquie and Don was to engage a daytime babysitter, to give them some relaxation time in the lead-up to an evening Date. If evenings prove too exhausting or problematic for you, the solution might be to plan a romantic day Date or even a two day weekend Date.

Stay Awake with the Daytime Date

Day Dates can be quite romantic really. Remember when you were first dating? Did you arrange trips to the beach, romantic picnics in a park, visits to a theme park or fair? Personally, I love a day out walking in the countryside or along the coast. I also highly rate a city Date, exploring new lunch venues and the latest art exhibitions. A full day together will find you slowing your step and finding time to express your thoughts. You'll find that you are more open to each other, and could learn more about your partner and they about you. (See Principle 10 to be prepared to *Reveal More*). Unless of course you arrange a 'movie fest' or day at the Formula One—both of which inhibit decent conversation! (Although fine for hand-holding.)

Going back to Peter; he did eventually admit that he and Layla used to be in the habit of planning a special day out for the other. They'd book the babysitter and take monthly turns to arrange a whole day with the other in mind. He shared with me how much joy he got from planning his special days for Layla, and it was nice to see the pleasure on his face as he recalled these Dates. I hope that they bring this habit back into their lives. Perhaps we all could be doing this.

If a whole day Date seems a bit ambitious, simply start with a morning Date. I have great memories of drawn-out breakfasts with Himself in our early dating days, as he ordered a lengthy smorgasbord of treats for my dining pleasure. Today we still indulge in the occasional breakfast, or more frequently, a brunch Date. A restaurant near where we lived in Hackney turned out a fabulous Sunday brunch. Located in a converted warehouse, we'd feel like we had retreated from the rest of the world. There was the oh-so rock 'n' roll leather-vested piano man, often still recovering from the night before, with old standards springing forth from his keys. Atop of his grand piano would be a mess of weekend papers. With the help of the music and perhaps a Bloody

Mary (yes, also on the menu) the idea of this Date was to enjoy our togetherness while unwinding and dispersing any tension from the working week just gone. In this retreat we'd spend an hour or two, musing on our blessings and playfully pondering our future. (See Principle 8 – *Toast Your Togetherness.*)

While our daytime Date may sound appealingly low-key, fitness enthusiast friends living in Dallas love a morning running Date. You might not find that romantic—but Dirk and Nally sure do! Dirk will plot new and scenic routes, they'll commune affectionately as they tick off the miles, enjoying the warmth of the rising sun and the cheerfulness of released endorphins. Afterwards they'll enjoy a picnic breakfast, seek out a local brunch recommendation, or indulge in a lavish home-cooked feast.

Guarantee Energy (& Romance) with the All-Weekend Date

Exhausted by the mere thought of a Date (even without the run)? If you have no real way of summoning energy before any Date, day or night, the two-night weekend break could be your dating solution. I understand that for many parents, a few hours away doesn't necessarily mean you can switch off and fully engage in and enjoy your Date. Will baby Polly be OK with the new babysitter? What's left in the refrigerator—should you pop into the supermarket on the way home? What is your teenager getting up to while you're out? With all these things ticking away in your mind, where's the energy to focus 100% on the Date? You surely can't expect a romantic outcome.

Romantic weekender Dates could be the best thing for you— whether you are parents, worn-out wage slaves, or just tired from other important commitments. Even if you're not *that* fatigued, add these extended Dates into your repertoire of possibilities, and do these at least three times a year. The first night should be a relaxed, low-key, recovery night, where you chill out and catch up on your beauty sleep, so that you are fully energised and ready for action for a Date Night the following evening.

Himself and I once stayed at a small country-house hotel, a short distance from Dublin. There arrived a smartly dressed couple in their late thirties, looking stressed and frazzled; their large people-moving wagon indicated parental responsibilities. As we shared with them our pre-dinner wine, we learnt that Maeve, a stay-at-home mum, and Connor, a charity executive, were taking a weekend break from their four children. They had purposely chosen the hotel for its convenience to their home, explaining they didn't want to waste precious time travelling, especially as they'd had to tour Dublin dispatching children to various family and friends. We also learnt that, sadly, their six-month-old was chronically ill.

Over the course of the weekend, we saw Maeve noticeably unwind. The initial hurried glasses of wine and the distracted eye contact was replaced by relaxed (and late) arrivals to breakfast, hand-in-hand walks to the lake, and laughter-filled piggyback rides across the estate. I was inspired by their marital commitment; in the face of crisis they were turning to, and nurturing, each other. If Maeve and Connor can summon energy for romance, then so can you.

But a weekender Date needn't involve the expense of a hotel or accommodation. Try arranging for the children to stay with family or friends while you have an 'at home' Date. If you'd rather go away to make the weekend even more special, but are worried about expense, consider staying with friends. Hark—can I hear you already exclaiming about the perceived problem with that? To avoid having a permanent escort, you *will* need to be upfront with your hosts about your romantic intention for the weekend. This is easier than you think. Simply say, "We would like some time to reconnect with each other, can we come and stay with you? It will be great to have dinner with you on the first night, but I'd like to treat the better half to a romantic meal on Saturday night. Can you recommend somewhere?" Or something like that. We've found this is not normally a problem; friends and family are generally willing contributors in the area of romance. I remember staying with Himself's best friend, Julian, in his apartment in Paris. Julian helped the romantic cause no end, from dispatching his personal driver to collect us at the airport, to letting us enjoy the rooftop terrace for hours on end without interruption. Have a think—is there someone who can fulfil this for you and your partner?

If you feel guilty about taking time away from your children, let me remind you of the good side. Children are sensitive to tensions, so ensuring a high level of relationship satisfaction helps to make a comfortable home for them. Also, if they see you valuing yourselves as a couple, you are being important role models for their own future relationships.

Actions:

- Figure out when you are likely to have the most energy for Date Night.
- Make sure a regular Date Night doesn't become a standard evening and lose its special spark. Mix it up by trying different venues and activities.
- Be sensitive to scheduling or commitment changes that can steal energy from your Date. It's better to postpone than to set up a Date for failure.
- Stifle yawns during Date Nights by arranging daytime Dates instead.
- Recharge your energy levels and boost your romance with a two-night weekend Date.
- Ask for help. Lots of people have a vested interest in your relationship health and are only too happy to lend a hand, whether babysitting, hosting a break, or providing you with some space.

So now you've learnt that the advantage of being an established couple is that you can *time* a Date Night with more chance of romantic success. Being aware of each other's weekly schedules—and beauty sleep rituals—means that you have good knowledge of whether a midweek or weekend Date will excel. You can figure out whether you are both going to be energised, and not under competing pressures, so that you are fully engaged and ready for action. That's a good start to an intimate event!

2. Book Your Table for Two

"Whenever I want a really nice meal, I start dating again."
— Susan Healy

Lesson from your early dates: When choosing your venue or activity, you'd plan how to hold their hand.

What would fan the flame of romance for you? Would it be the modern lighting and funky décor of a chic inner city bar, or a candle-lit French bistro? Perhaps lying side by side, towelling-robed in a day spa, as your feet are massaged in unison? Would your hearts melt while watching a nature documentary or a romantic comedy? Would your pulses pump going dog racing or salsa dancing?

Our surroundings influence us all, whether we're conscious of it or not. We can choose our settings to suit our objectives. In my work as a psychologist for example: if I'm facilitating a conflict-resolution session, I'm hardly going to meet the disputing parties in a rowdy pub environment. No, I'll take them to a serene, zen-like hotel. If I want a group to be more creative, then I'll find a not-so-ordinary venue in a vibrant area.

Likewise, since the intention of Date Night is romance, consider a venue that is romantic in itself, or at least supports the specialness of the occasion, which is the essence of this Principle – *Book Your Table for Two*. But don't feel you have to be limited to this. You can still choose a Date activity or venue that is not terribly romantic by nature, but you will need to make more of an effort to create an intimate mood. At the end of this chapter I have some thoughts on how you can inject some spark into the least romantic of activities.

The Utterly Romantic Venue

This is where the Date setting, scene and activity are in themselves romantic. That is, the very event or scene brings about a tender sensuality and heightened sense of intimacy—and yes, here is where the clichéd romantic settings fit in. Candle-lit dining on intimate balconies under a star-lit sky, soft music and stunning views, slow dancing and a sunset cruise, a private stroll through an extensive landscaped garden (the common setting for romance in Jane Austen's era). Naturally, these surroundings perfectly set the tone for Date Night.

If you want to be a little less clichéd, or if the above settings are out of your reach, think about and investigate what might appeal to the romantic sentiments in you and your partner. I love it when Himself, who doesn't cook as a rule, prepares me a simple fish supper. To add the element of romance, the dining table will be adorned with candles and wine served in our finest glasses. I am enamoured. For this evening, the world is just Himself and Me.

Keep in mind that not all the clichéd settings deliver romance. Take, for instance, my friend Cynthia's Date Night fiasco. She had whisked her husband Clive across the English Channel to Amsterdam for a romantic weekend break, and organised a Date Night at a new restaurant called 'Supper Club'. At this intimate venue, all diners reclined and ate on what could only be described as a massive bed; a single raised mattress that spanned the walls in a U-shape. In case you're imagining some dodgy opium den, this is a high-end restaurant, with a price tag that would rival only the best. The experience however, Cynthia told me with a raised eyebrow, was not quite what they expected. The restaurant took mood lighting to a whole new level; the menu could barely be read by the flame of a candle. A romantic, even sexy, dining experience for some people—but 'some people' did not include Clive. He was disturbed by not being able to see what he was eating, or the fellow diners (in this case, fellow bed mates). Cynthia did learn something that evening however. Clive revealed that he does find Lebanese-style restaurants romantic; those un-modernised establishments where old men can be found out front smoking apple pipes or playing backgammon, and inside a cosy room with plump and plentiful cushions for seats, and low but 'can-still-read-the-menu' lighting. For a future Date, Cynthia will go for the real thing.

Take time to discover what settings and activities inspire a romantic feeling, and evaluate a proposed activity's potential to do this. You're not always going to see eye-to-eye on some activities. Himself considers a barefoot stroll along a long beach to be romantic, whereas I find traversing a never-ending expanse of sand to be the last word in tedium. Yet we both enjoy the romance of a walk through tranquil countryside and picturesque villages. Have a chat with your partner, explore romantic memories and see what you can discover. You might be surprised.

What are your Special Places and Doings?

The most unlikely events or venues can be meaningful to a couple. The

British pie and mash shop, its aged formica tables littered with refuse from previous diners, might seem quite the opposite of romantic. But for Sally and Pete, a nursery teacher and surveyor married twenty-one years, this is where they were first introduced. The occasional pie with mash at this venue brings up romantic memories of eyes meeting across the mushy peas, and generates a sense of closeness and connection (and hopefully not indigestion).

For Alison and Tim, married thirty-three years, attending a concert by 1970's folk group Fairport Convention is the epitome of romance. For many years, 'White Dress' by the group has been their song. When it comes to anniversaries or the occasional at-home Date Night, they'll have a slow dance to this tune; I believe Alison even puts on a white dress.

Frederica revealed that she and Roger were looking forward to a Date to see the latest *Star Trek* movie. I must have looked surprised; I couldn't imagine sci-fi inspiring a romantic quality other than holding a partner's hand in cinema darkness. She quenched my curiosity, explaining that they can trace their long-standing marriage through the ongoing adventures of Captain Kirk and the crew of the Federation Star Ship Enterprise. Through Frederica I learnt that there may be a special romantic aura to many a planetary or fantasy world, for folk who have met their spouse through fandoms.

Elevate your Date

Seek out a venue or activity that is remarkable in itself, and obviously not part of your weekly ritual. This will elevate your Date! If you eat out twice a week at your local restaurant, and you also make this your Date setting, what is there to signify your Date Night as special? See what I mean?

Although there are a further 15 Principles covered in this book, this is an important one. Behavioural psychologists agree that the environment gives the subconscious mind cues on how to behave[3]. You might have observed small children behaving radically different depending on whether they're at home or at Granny's house. A change in scene can cause you to be more deliberate and thoughtful with your actions and behaviour. A Date Night is focused on romance, so rather than your regular haunt where you'd meet up with mates or simply satisfy your hunger, go elsewhere to a setting that's new, out-of-the-ordinary and special.

If you are regular cinema-goers, a standard movie night can be elevated to romantic levels if you've booked opening night tickets to a much anticipated sequel, as Frederica did. Or try booking the movie of your partner's choice at a 'Gold Class' cinema (if your city is lucky enough to have one) where you sit in comfy recliners with waiter service right to your seats.

A Purely Unromantic Venue—Made Special

With forethought, creative thinking and a little research, you can inject romance into almost any activity! As mentioned earlier, your romantic evening is easier if the environment hints at romance. If it doesn't, you'll then need to exert more effort to bring in that romantic or special element. Himself is always teasing me that he'll take me on a Date to the greyhound races. I must admit the mere thought makes me shudder; I have an unpleasant image of standing around getting cold, eating greasy flaccid chips, surrounded by men in old-fashioned overcoats, hat brims pulled down as they mutter tips to each other. Yet my notion of 'going to the dogs' could be romantic if we invested in making the occasion special. This could involve VIP tickets, booking a table at a restaurant or viewing gallery, then getting dressed up, arriving in style, a glass of bubbly and so on. Then again, you could discard any need for glitz and glamour, and simply fix affectionate wagers before each race. (Although Himself and I do love our glitz and glamour.)

Then there is Angus. Proud of his engineering profession, Angus suggested to his partner that they have Date Night at the HQ for the Institution of Civil Engineers. His fun-loving partner Milly was stifling yawns at the mere prospect of an evening spent in an archaic building. And a Date Night at that! Yet Angus is no fool and had chosen well. Often used as a wedding venue, the beautiful interior featured oak panelling and lit chandeliers. He had made special arrangements that included taking Milly for a private behind-the-scenes tour, ending with fine food and wine in the Institution's prestigious restaurant. But what Milly most remembers about the evening is the intimacy of the stories Angus shared as they toured the building... how he used the library when he was studying for his exams, which rooms he had lectures in, who he had met where, his graduation and so on. She felt a stronger sense of connection with him. And he with her.

So rest assured—even the seemingly least romantic of settings can be redeemed. At least I fully believe so, and to test this, I scraped the edges of my imagination to conjure the least romantic and uninspiring venue for a Date and then to reflect on the means and ways it could be saved. Of the daunting Date prospects, I figure watching commercial aircraft take-off and land would score well on *my* 'uninspiring stakes'. We once lived near an airport and I was always bemused at the number of plane spotters, sitting in their cars on a bleak section of tarmac beside a highway, craning their necks to see the aircraft beyond. Such an activity could be transformed with meaningful memories about trips past, dreaming together of future trips, favourite mood music on the car stereo, a lovingly prepared hamper of gourmet snacks, and a car rug to snuggle under.

The Importance of Comfort

No matter how romantic the venue is, without comfort all can be ruined. I could give you numerous examples from our dating history where Date Night lost its romantic spark due to discomfort suffered by one or both of us. Such as the intimate wine bar and restaurant that surprised us with bar stools that were incredibly, both bottom-numbing and back-breaking (perhaps their tactic for a quick turnover of patrons). Or the night we spent more than an hour competing with the post-theatre crowd for a cab home—we were eventually defeated. So rather than cosying up to Himself in a cab, I had to get close-up and personal with post-pub drunks strap-hanging in a crowded night bus.

At the heart of the issue, a lack of comfort can translate to discontentment or distraction. Either way, they don't bode well for success on Date Night.

Come to know what comfort means for your Date Night. For Himself, after many nights painstakingly seeking cabs, he loves being walking distance from home. With his bad back, he also prefers cushioned seating at a restaurant. I like nothing more than being able to have a seat whilst enjoying a pre-dinner drink. My willingness to stand at a bar ended along with my twenties. Meanwhile, our friend Andrew has a hearing impairment so it's essential for him that he can be seated with his back against a wall. (His accommodating wife jokingly proposes that it's his plot to get the best view of the room.)

By now, you are either thinking 'what a bunch of oldies!' or you are nodding sagely, relating to these dilemmas. But comfort-seeking isn't the domain only of the aging. Even a twenty-two-year-old will have some comfort requirements. Take my younger sister. In her twenties, she had the *MTV* Generation short attention span, so any cinema or theatre event that lasted more than eighty minutes would send her quite literally to sleep. You see? Once you understand your own essential needs, you can accommodate these with a bit of planning and forethought.

Sometimes, despite the best laid plans, you are going to get caught out. I had secured a table at a new French bistro in the city. I double-checked its romantic and comfort credentials on the Internet, and sure enough there were lush furnishings—padded seating for Himself—and the décor had an intimate retro feel. On a cold autumnal evening we arrived red-nosed and looking forward to warming ourselves inside. It quickly became apparent that a brisk breeze was going to be a feature of the evening: waiters were serving a table of diners who were seated outside under gas heaters. The size of the group required a door to be permanently open, which brought about an indoor-outdoor dining experience for everyone. As you'll soon see in Principle 7 – *Every Venue Has a Silver Lining*, it's important to remain positive despite imperfections. So we put a brave face on the evening and Himself even showed his feminine side by sharing my pashmina for respite from the fresh conditions. Needless to say we didn't stay long, with the lack of hot desserts also fast-tracking our exit. It was an OK evening but it failed to score on the romantic stakes. Comfort is crucial—without it, there is a limited chance of romance on a Date. If I could push rewind, I would have politely upped-sticks and relocated to a neighbouring brasserie—fully-enclosed with radiator pumping.

Actions:

- Choose a Date Night venue that is romantic in itself.
- Keep a note of what you both find romantic, as this will help if you get stuck for Date ideas.
- Look for events and places that have significance in your relationship.
- Be creative—take an activity that's not otherwise romantic, and make it special.

- Become aware of your core comfort requirements, and learn to accommodate them.
- Turn to page 179 for *Date Idea-Sparkers* — a full evaluation of many popular Date activities.

Your lesson here boils down to this: don't underestimate the influence of your environment! You want to push those tender feeling buttons, invoke sensuality and a heightened sense of intimacy, so there's no place for ordinary on a Date Night. So when you *Book Your Table for Two*, select your setting and scene to score on the romantic stakes. If it's not romantic in itself, then make sure it's meaningful or special.

3. Find Your Date Night Finery

"A woman is closest to being naked when she is well-dressed."
— Coco Chanel

Lesson from your early dates: You made a determined effort *not* to put them off!

If you were out to woo your husband, seduce your wife or significant other, would you wear that favourite, old, homemade cardigan? You know the one—oh so comfy but oh so shapeless? Come on—of course you wouldn't. And if you would, you really need this Principle.

Whatever the nature of the Date, be it a sports event, movie night or an intimate meal, you should always put some thought and effort into looking your best. Even if you've organised an 'at home' Date, this does *not* give you permission to stay in your track pants or comfortable cargos. Making a special effort with your appearance helps to set this evening apart from just any old evening, and lets your partner know that you have romance on your mind. Your second-best pair of jeans isn't going to cut it.

Think back to when you were on the single scene. Even for an intimate supper Date at home, you would have spruced yourself up a bit, maybe applied a scent of the masculine or feminine persuasion, preened your hair, dressed in something a little special. Now in an established relationship, your partner may have seen you 'au natural' for many years, but that's no excuse for not putting in some extra effort on Date Night.

At this point, I'm not going to prescribe that you should wear a fashionable skirt, iron your shirt or even polish your shoes—because what makes you attractive 'is in the eye of the beholder'; what makes you feel confident is unique to you. Consider this story about Karen and Brian, married ten years and living in San Francisco with a beloved old dog. Brian is a scientist and part-time artist who fosters a counter-establishment look. Whilst he's long since ceased to sport the long hair, he insists on wearing creased clothes and manages a convincing unkempt look, to the frustration of his smartly dressed wife and their housekeeper who happens to like ironing. (Yes, such people do exist.) When Brian and Karen stayed with us in Ireland I could sense Karen's annoyance in Brian's shabby presentation. Yet their attraction is based on his challenging and alternative perspectives, which is reflected in his dress. Now I normally remain an observer in these issues, but in this case, I came up with a quick fix: as we were about to set off to a designer restaurant, I suggested that Brian try one of Himself's trilbies. This jauntily perched hat transformed the shabby scientist to hip yet alternative fashionista. Brian wasn't compromising his identity, there were no ironed shirts, and he looked fabulous. Karen was clearly delighted in the new look, clinging to him on our walk to the restaurant (or was that the high heels I loaned her?). Although Brian's a long way from becoming the Mad Hatter, I hear Karen has lured him into a men's milliner to further activate this minimal yet striking makeover.

What Do you Both find Attractive?

Your Date Night presentation is not about being the most fashionable, trendy or even being, as in Brian's case, 'true to yourself'. It's really about making yourself optimally attractive to your mate. Yes, that's right. So if they think your Ugg boots should never be seen past the front door, you are going to kiss those warm woolly interiors bye-bye for the evening, and slip on those heels that add a sexy wriggle to your walk.

Some couples, like our friends Dean and James, get dressed together for Date Night and other special occasions. It's part of their ritual of intimacy for the evening; they actively help each other choose a look, covering everything from clothes and shoes to cologne and hair style, all in a spirit of openness, patience and mutual respect. If you are such a couple who get dressed together, then you're lucky. You can both leave the house confidently knowing that your partner finds you supremely attractive. Why not try introducing co-dressing as part of your Dating preparation? It may not suit all individuals—those who are more private, less patient or less enthused by the dressing process, may prefer not to. But not to worry, there are plenty of ways to uncover what your significant other finds most appealing on you (pun not intended—this is about putting clothes *on!*).

What Does your Mate find Attractive About your Look?

My man isn't the trendiest guy on the block. Attempting to get his heart pattering by wearing the latest edgy Vogue fashions would be a waste of time. Thankfully Himself is upfront with what he finds attractive and what he doesn't. Intimidating for some! But I take comfort in the transparency of his opinion. (I don't even need to *ask* his opinion, it will be offered automatically.)

What if your spouse isn't quite so forthcoming as Himself? We know the 'correct' answer to "Does my bum look big in this?" is "Of course not, dear". But what if they suggest that *everything* in your wardrobe is perfectly fine? Don't believe them! They're either being lazy, or don't know how to express what they like on you—but they will find *something* attractive. You'll need to channel your inner Sherlock Holmes to discover what this is. These suggestions will help your investigation:

- Give them limited choices. You'll have more luck asking "Do you prefer me in this outfit or that?" than if you throw open a wardrobe bulging with outfits, announcing "What would you like me to wear?" The key to this discussion is to make it light-hearted, and that any answer is OK. Let me repeat that—any answer is OK. If the air is emotionally charged and you get defensive about the answers, you are not likely to get the truth now or in the future.

- Use fashion spreads or magazine advertisements to prompt a discussion about trends and styles. Best to select one or two pages for their review; don't overwhelm them by shoving a whole magazine under their nose.

- Go through your photo collections and ask them to identify their favourite look from your history together.

- Make the most of people-watching together, whether it's at Starbucks, a sports event, your local restaurant or church, and ask your mate to point out one outfit that could look good on you. If you're feeling brave, you can ask the wearer of the outfit where they bought it. I have trained Himself to do this.

- Find time to shop together and you will quickly glean their opinion. It's important though to be open to your mate's honesty, and to let them be honest without a backlash. Some years ago when I fell in love with a cream skirt, Himself suggested I needed a larger size. Whilst I didn't wish to talk to him for a week, I valued his truthfulness. You'll also want to assure their comfort while shopping together. Himself has a short attention span for clothes shopping, so I only take him to see my 'top picks' where, while I'm in the changing room, he can comfortably sit with other men wearing long-suffering faces.

• Let your significant other buy you an outfit of their choosing. The process of them selecting clothes for you can be revealing, as you can discover what shapes, colours, textures they find attractive on you. Take note of comments like "this shows off your legs" or "it looks feminine/manly on you" (gender-appropriate, of course), "blue is your colour" and so on. All good data to remember for future Date Nights.

Once you have this valuable information tucked away, you can then make informed decisions when preparing for Date Night. For example, having once cut my hair in a short bob, I learnt that Himself actually likes my hair slightly longer. This enables me to put my hair 'up', thereby—as he informed me—accentuating my nape and the graceful length of my neck. Now that's good to know. Yet I know most of my friends consider my 'up-do' too severe for my face and personality. On Date Night however, guess who wins. With romantic intent in mind, I'll happily put my hair up, confident that Himself will appreciate it and find it sexy.

This isn't all one way, of course. Remember to communicate what *you* find attractive. For instance, Himself has a spotted-shirt and checked-tie combination that he sometimes wears to work, which I believe he associates fondly with appearing the eccentric Englishman. I, however, take exception to this outfit on Date Night—I'm the one who has to sit opposite it! For a number of years I tried to overlook his choice of attire, scolding myself at such superficial thoughts; telling myself "this is the man of my life. I love him and his foibles". The reality is that *visual attraction* is a key element to the courting game. Be honest to yourself and your partner about what you find most attractive on them. Don't put up with eye-sores that are a turn-off. That will not help the romance at all!

Ladies, do you love seeing your man in a tailored suit if he meets you directly from the office? Do you like him in jeans and fitted shirt on a weekend Date? Be sure to let him know.

How can you best communicate what you find attractive?

- Let them know, whenever they wear something that ticks your boxes, how much you appreciate their good taste. If it's worn on a non-Date Night, suggest it would make a great Date Night outfit.
- Point out outfits that you find attractive on other people, suggesting that it would look good on them.
- Note shop window displays with items that would look sexy on them. People are generally flattered if you've been thinking of them while shopping.
- Cut out pages from magazines and newspapers that feature pleasing apparel.
- Be truthful about physical oversights. We can all be oblivious at times, some of us are more absent-minded than others, and may not notice physical changes that are unattractive. It could be a lush growth of nostril hair, an unsightly mole hair, a straggly eyebrow or pending mono-brow, a fake tan that looks like they've been glazed in Fanta. Think how you can sensitively encourage them to address these oversights. For example, a friend on her way to the dermatologist for her annual mole check got a call from her husband. Firstly he wished her luck for the visit and then, as if an afterthought, suggested that whilst she was there, perhaps she could remove the skin tag near her eyelid, as it looked, in some lights, like a pimple. (This was news to her but, needless to say, the spot was promptly snipped.) Some people might be more responsive to playful humour: "Honey, your nostril hair will soon be dipping in the soup!"
- Share if clothes are too short or simply worn past their best. Kindly suggest that if they like it, by all means wear it, but perhaps not on Date Night. Himself knows that I don't like trousers to be too short in the leg, he has some favourite smart jeans which he loves which

are a tad too short, grazing his ankle in a less-than-fashionable way (at least, not fashionable at the time of writing! You never know...) He still wears them, just not on Date Night.

A word of warning. Refrain from consistently selecting and laying out clothes for them to wear! Be honest, partners of reluctant or bad dressers, you were thinking of doing that, weren't you? Unlike our good examples Dean and James, the couple who choose outfits together in mutual respect, a one-way dictation of what the other wears can come across as controlling and patronising. And for men, this can be emasculating. What's more, you'd be stifling their opportunity to dress for you, and to develop their own thought and consideration for Date Night. By all means, if invited to offer an opinion or to select an outfit as a one-off exercise, share your preferences but don't be insistent. Remember on page 56, I suggested letting your partner buy you an outfit? That is a data collection exercise to find out what they find attractive on you, and if doing it in return for your partner, make sure it is a welcome or invited activity.

Fashion-conscious Freya was far too enthusiastic. When seriously involved with Brendon for several years, she was proud to have a man who could wear clothes well. She would shop for him, buying suits, shirts and ties and even a kilt(!) to co-ordinate him perfectly for parties, weddings, Dates and other such events. Yes folks, Brendon was more of an accessory than a date. It seemed Brendon suspected this as well. Although he never suggested that he would rather dress himself, he simply one day told Freya that he was packing his Gucci man-bag and moving on. Possibly to live ever-after in comfy track pants.

Don't Spring any Surprises on Date Night

You might be loving your new crocodile-skin jacket or Dame Edna Everidge glasses, a statement-making new eyebrow piercing, or platinum blondness after being a brunette. It's too easy to assume that something *you* love will be loved by your partner too. However, if you haven't done the prior research with your mate, I'd warn you against launching a new look on Date Night. Guys, this is not the time to reveal a 'number one' scalp shave if your sweetheart loves the way your hair curls on your collar.

Dublin-based Daria tells me about a birthday occasion, where she put on a new brown suede outfit that she was saving for the event. On her proud descent down the stairs, husband Monty commented that she was dressing like his mother. Needless to say, this knocked her confidence and almost any potential for romance on the evening. She may have fared better if she'd tried on the outfit earlier to gauge his reaction.

There's little doubt that the familiarity of being in a couple can result in taking each other for granted. Certainly on Date Night, you want to whisk off that old cloak of familiarity and make the evening special, but be careful about shedding *too much*. You don't want to frighten your poor partner out of their wits, or have them sitting there uncomfortably wondering what possessed you to wear a neon-pink jumpsuit.

I'm not one for wearing much make-up; I've always preferred a relatively natural look and simply use a little foundation and lipstick. However, as age creeps up on a girl, she may feel compelled to do battle with nature. As my mother says, "If the barn needs painting, paint it." Before one Date Night, I booked in for a makeover. The result was dramatic: I didn't recognise myself in the heavy eye makeup and tanned foundation! Himself was clearly alarmed by the new look, then tactfully and playfully directed me to the ladies bathroom to remove it. Hint taken. I must have been expecting this reaction—I was able to calmly rationalise with him that I would like to retain the new face for the rest of the evening, and to see if we could get used to it. Ironically, that very night we were photographed for the society pages of *Irish Tatler*. At least I got some value out of that makeover. But that's how *I* learned to save the trialling of a new me for a non Date Night evening.

So remember this lesson: if you are trying something new, find out whether it's attractive to them *before* Date Night. If you simply don't have time to, and if they initially don't like the change, ask them to be generous spirited and see whether the new look grows on them during your Date. They may be surprised.

Make Sure you Feel Confident

What do you enjoy wearing with confidence?

Three inch heels does it for me. I wear three inchers because they make me feel confident, sexy and powerful. I like the way they lengthen my legs and transform my walk; I feel emboldened by the sound of them on hardwood floors or reverberating on polished concrete as they announce my arrival. And then, as they make me feel confident, my behaviours during an evening are transformed. I am more positive and find myself being more giving and more attentive to my partner. This means I will be improving my score on several other Date Night Principles.

Confidence in how you look can bolster self-esteem and this is vital for a successful evening. Let's say you just put on a favourite outfit— but what's this? You feel uncomfortable. Maybe you've changed shape, maybe fashion has changed shape. Maybe that hem line suddenly seems a little too high, or that skin-tight shirt a little too tight.

So wear something else! If you feel uncomfortable, you are compromising the potential of the evening. Perhaps you are most self-conscious about your hair. Does it get bouffy, develop a frizz halo or go limp, or does the wind transform you into a scarecrow? You're not alone there. On the more extravagant Date Nights I like to bully mine into place with a professional blow-dry. And it's not unusual to witness Himself hightailing it to the barber in the hours leading up to our Date! Be it hair or heels or the clothing in between—what's important to you?

I asked a few female friends what makes them feel confident on a

Date Night. The common response? Lingerie.

Ah yes, the naughty, the lacy, the frilly, the frivolous, the crisp, the colourful. Donning a more suggestive set of undergarments boosts their confidence, I'm told, and helps to put them in the mood for romance. During my childhood I was bemused by television advertisements for a local lingerie brand. Suburban yummy mummies radiated contentment whilst doing ordinary household chores: pushing prams, hanging out the laundry and collecting the post while the slogan purred: "It's not what's on the outside, it's what you wear underneath". Can you relate to that? Many can. In Dubai, a city where it's customary for local women to wear the full-covering *abaya,* the saucy high-end lingerie label *Agent Provocateur* has apparently become a massive hit. Women are not alone in pursuing underclothing confidence; men's magazines advertise sports stars in low-cut boxer shorts or fitted y-fronts. The 'bottom' line is, if wearing sexy underwear or lingerie makes you feel good, then invest in a special set. Go on, you know you want to! Your partner benefits from your enhanced self-esteem and may have the added pleasure of sensually removing them from your person, at some point in the proceedings.

As mentioned earlier, confidence can fundamentally affect the tone and nature of the Date. If you allow a lack of self-esteem to accompany you, you're more prone to being defensive and negative (Principle 12 – *Negativity No-Nos*), and might find it difficult to engage in good Date etiquette. As well as not starting the night in good spirits by failing to *Arrive 'in Smile'* (Principle 4) and being downbeat about the setting (Principle 7 – *Every Venue Has a Silver Lining*), you could find yourself withdrawing from Principles like *Toast Your Togetherness* (Principle 8), *The Etiquette of Flattery* (Principle 9) and *Reveal More* (Principle 10). Physical attraction may be a cornerstone of your relationship, but *confidence* is the facilitator of your Date Night. Think of confidence as your 'chaperone', keeping you on your best Date Night behaviour.

Actions:

- Pay extra attention to your appearance; it will mark Date Night as special.
- Dress to impress your partner. And do your research—it's crucial to avoid wearing anything they dislike.
- Positively reinforce what you find attractive on your partner.
- Address any physical oversights: theirs and your own. But don't be over zealous: nasal hair is one thing but rhinoplasty is another!
- Be careful not to surprise them by launching a new look on Date Night as this could misfire.
- Dress for confidence, to bolster your self-esteem. This is sure to improve your all-round Date performance.

Academic psychologists, exploring the law of attraction, have researched how single people perceive potential mates. Did you know that within a half second, singletons will fix on who they consider the most physically attractive person?[4] *Half a second*. Gives new meaning to the well-known counsel that 'first impressions count'! Linking physical presentation with 'potential mate' desirability is all the evidence a singleton needs to realise the importance of their own appearance.

Unfortunately, there's considerably less research on how this law of attraction evolves once in established relationships. So while the academics get on with it, let us sum up the evident benefits of dressing to impress the mate you've selected some time ago: making an effort with your appearance on Date Night is an important signal to your mate that this is a special night. This effort reinforces the romantic intent of the evening. By dressing in a way that your partner loves, you are communicating your thoughtfulness and your respect for them. Also, feeling good about how you look can have an uplifting effect on your confidence; and the self-assurance that comes from this will have a knock-on positive effect on all parts of the Date.

4. Arrive 'in Smile'

*"Let us always meet each other with a smile,
for the smile is the beginning of love."*
— Mother Teresa

Lesson from your early dates: No bad moods allowed!

You're grumpy at the taxi driver who's assumed you're a tourist, clocking up the fare by taking you the scenic route. You've just spotted a coffee stain on your shirt. You feel irked by a phone call from your sister about the fight she had with your mother. Your shoes are already pinching, there's a run in your brand new tights, and the evening's hardly begun. You're moments away from meeting your partner on Date Night. Will you let these niggling annoyances cloud your mood? Will you simply have to have a moan as soon as you get there?

Despite the best intentions to *Arrive 'in Smile'*, we can all be unsettled by events in the hours leading up to meeting on Date Night.

63

Some things could be foreseen, others might completely be outside your control, as if you've been targeted by the bad luck fairy.

Edgy about work? Maybe Date Night is causing you to miss an impromptu meeting; a trusted colleague has just resigned; or as you were leaving the office you were painfully reminded of your forthcoming performance appraisal. Or is something brewing in your household affairs? An overdue credit card bill, a missed call from the school, a heating malfunction... there are oodles of reasons why we can be fully and justifiably grumpy when meeting our mate. But remember: Date Night isn't just any evening. With its focus on romantic intent, you'll be wanting to make the other person feel valued, appreciated and special. Indeed, studies show that when you are in a positive mood you are more likely to feel closer and more attracted to your partner.[5] Starting the Date from a position of low spirits will make harder work of achieving your romantic objective. Just think of another situation where you'd put your best foot forward to achieve a goal—a job interview. You're hardly going to start *that* with a frown and a whinge about the blister from your new shoes!

Why does this Principle feature in the Manifesto? Surely it's a *given* that one arrives at any event in good spirits? Well, it's here because *I* have simply killed too many Date Nights by arriving in a state that has condemned the evening from the get-go. Much like the disastrous Date that sparked off the birth of the Date Night Manifesto, I have screeds of these Dates on record. Romance has bitten the dust because my out-of-sorts starting condition has rendered me off-kilter, prickly, even angst-ridden, for the rest of the night. In this chapter I'll discuss how you can maximise your chances of arriving in an auspicious mood. I will cover both the heads and tails of the good spirits coin: on one side what you can include in your day that you know you'll enjoy, and on the other, how to insulate yourself against negative elements which are sure to irritate or frustrate. I'll also address how you can save the Date when a case of sheer bad luck threatens to chase good spirits away.

Smile Brighteners

First of all, let's figure out what you can do to arrive in your best frame of mind, with a smile on your dial, assuring your good spirits. What is likely to have a mood-enhancing effect for you?

For me, if I've indulged myself with something new or fun that day, such as popping into an art exhibition at lunchtime or catching up with a friend, then I'm normally a far happier date. If it's a work day, I find that after I've been facilitating meetings or workshops, I'm upbeat and 'buzzed' which also makes for a great date. If you're the sort of person who likes to clear your in-tray and completely tick off your checklist on any given day, then go easy on the number of chores you assign yourself on the day of a Date. There's no need to orchestrate potential distress and discontentment; a shorter list may heighten your sense of personal control and satisfaction.

"But hang on," you say, "my time is *always* hectic, on a *normal* day!" If possible, you might want to postpone a meeting or activity so the afternoon at least is more relaxed and less stressful. If your diary is outside your control and you often end the day feeling as drained as an empty bathtub, build in some unwind time before meeting for a Date. Try not to rush straight from work to the venue! Taking time out to discharge the pressures and stresses can yield dividends for both you and your spouse. For some people a quiet read of a favourite magazine or an indulgent bubble bath will do the trick; for others it could be browsing in a music shop or having a quick half-pint with colleagues and friends. My friend Emma likes to book herself a facial. The self-indulgence and time-out from the office grind and daily duties helps her unwind and puts her in a blissful state of mind for her Date.

Exercise is the great unwinder for others; the release of endorphins really sets them on the 'good spirits' path. I can recognise a significant change in Himself's demeanour if he has completed a full yoga session—he radiates an underlying contentment, which bodes well for the romantic intentions of the evening. A word of warning on strenuous sporting endeavours; don't overdo it before a Date. Obviously it's not a good idea to expend the last of your energy on the exercise that's supposed to be setting you up for a good evening. (See Principle 1 – *Get Your Beauty Sleep,* for the importance of energy on a Date.) I am an avid long distance runner, and after some astute observation, Himself concluded that my undertaking a run on the day of a Date Night compromised my 'in Smile' arrival. He swears that 'post-run me' greets him with a weak grin and sallow face (gee thanks darling!) and that's before he gets started on my elderly pace.

Speaking of Himself, work can significantly enhance his mood; presenting to an audience often has an exhilarating effect on his spirit. What enthuses you? When are you likely to be at your best? Can you incorporate any of these activities in the day leading to a Date?

Farewell those Frowns

On the flipside of the coin, what could constitute your personal recipe for disaster? Are there any pre-Date events or activities that are could negatively impact the start of the evening? Gillian booked a detox massage and body wrap before a gastronomic Date Night, not realising the nature of the detox could bring about nausea, and she should avoid alcohol and food. Oops! Hardly an ideal start for a culinary extravaganza of a Date Night; however, she did say her husband Greg enjoyed her portions as well as his own. Another personal example: Himself is a fervent follower of Liverpool FC and they happened to be playing the same evening as a planned Date Night. Not wanting Himself to miss the game, I organised pre-dinner drinks at a pub where he could watch the end of the football match on their large sports screen. But it didn't occur to me what would happen to our Date. I can now put forward this equation: poor football score = deflated mood = poor Date Night score!

So whilst I avoid long distance runs and Himself avoids the football scores, we are both mindful of work issues that can negatively impact the evening. For the working day leading up to a Date Night, I find myself scheduling any potentially troublesome meetings for other days. I have even postponed reading emails from an irksome client, to do away with possible frustration. I figure that digesting a problematic 4pm email at 8am the next day is unlikely to make that much difference to the client, and it insulates me and importantly the Date from an irritated start! Getting an irritation-loaded email at the end of a workday can upset the apple cart. If despite best intentions, you do read a troublesome email— it was marked 'urgent', or gave the misleading appearance of being 'safe'—mentally practise shelving it. Don't let it spoil your evening.

Himself simply avoids it altogether by turning off any email device a good hour or so before a Date, so that there aren't any nasty surprises that might trouble him. I also notice that if we have a Saturday Date, he resists opening any of the morning post, saying he doesn't wanted to be annoyed by changes in mortgage rates, or a hike in utility bills. If these things frustrate you, see if you too can save it for later.

Got children? Arriving zen-like for Date Night might seem rather idealistic, yes? With some thought and creativity, you can create an auspicious start to your Date. Suzy and Gordon, parents of two energetic toddlers, found they could lower their collective blood pressure by securing the babysitter for an extra hour before the Date. The sitter takes care of baths and bedtime reading rituals, allowing Suzy and Gordon to get ready in peace, thus dodging bedtime battles and bath time splashes on their Date Night attire. Belinda and Patrick, parents of teenagers, have also discovered ways of avoiding pre-Date stress. Finding it hurried and awkward to cook dinner for their sons and prepare for Date Night, Belinda and Patrick have allocated their Date Night as the boys' cooking night. So whilst sons Michael and Kieran finetune their favourite recipes, Mum and Dad can finish their Date Night prep in peace.

Arriving with a smile and in good spirits can also be connected to self-esteem. It goes without saying, really—if you're not feeling confident, you're not likely to be in top form. So whatever you do, make sure you do *not* engage in activities that'll play havoc with your confidence levels. Pre-Date is not the ideal time to try on a skimpy bikini, jump on the scales, try to wheedle a bonus out of a new boss, or experiment with a new haircut that you end up hating. (See Principle 3 – *Find Your Date Night Finery* for more information on dressing confidently.) These things could trigger low self-esteem, which in turn triggers the moodiness you want to avoid.

Most Dates require some travel time. Even an 'at home' Date, on a week day, may require the journey from work. Since the journey often immediately precedes a Date, it can be a major contributor to your pre-Date spirits. Just travel *itself*—from being stuck behind the wheel in a gridlock, to making like a sardine on public transport—can have us snarling under our breath. So give extra thought to your 'to-the-Date' travel arrangements. You want to be really mindful of reducing any journey-induced angst or frustration. Are you a tense driver who frequently gets worked up driving in peak hour traffic? Are you even prone to—dare I say it—road rage? Think about the success of the Date being your priority and perhaps choose not to drive. Let yourself be collected, get a lift with a work colleague, take a train, or simply depart earlier to avoid the rush hour.

Let me tell you about an occasion where we were in France and taking the tram to our Date location. I had suggested taking a cab, given we were on unfamiliar turf, to reduce any journey stress. However, Himself insisted on the tram; he has a thing about rail systems, so for him navigating the trams was a stimulating start to a Date. We ended up taking a number of trams, going in every direction except where we needed to go—which was perhaps Himself's cunning plan to explore all the lines. I found myself tottering behind him, risking life and limb on my three inch heels, jumping tracks between onward coming cars and buses to catch yet another tram. I was at the point of mutiny, when we happened upon the correct tram. The peaceful remainder of the journey; the gentle motion of the tram, the quiet carriage and city views swept away our ill-fated start and we arrived a picture of calm—luckily for us, as our collective mood could otherwise have been quite jittery. Identifying the correct tram route in advance would have been a nice idea—or simply taking a cab.

So do your homework. If you are travelling to a new location, do your checks, use your map, the internet or your Sat-Nav. Calling the venue in advance for directions, transport options and parking is also sensible. There's no excuse for a poorly thought-out route on a Date Night!

Here's how a stressful journey bringing about a late and uncomfortable arrival can send a person (namely me!) off-kilter on a Date Night. A much-anticipated Date had been arranged at a most exclusive and acclaimed Dublin steakhouse. Given the significant expense of the smallest 6oz sirloin, I recognised that this could well be our once-in-our-lifetime visit, so I was determined to make it a night to remember. (It was, but not in the way I hoped.) I spent *hours* musing over what to wear, where to meet and how to style my hair. I carefully examined their online menu and reviews to decide on their signature side options (asparagus and onion strings, it so happened). On the day, I was surprised and disappointed to discover it was blowing a gale, with intermittent downpours of rain. This was sure to make my budget-saving walk and rail journey to meet Himself at the restaurant a little precarious. Yet I shouldn't have been surprised; after all we lived in Dublin where it has been known to rain every day of the summer. At some romantic level I must have imagined only the finest of weather would manifest itself for our sumptuous evening. I armed myself with an umbrella and timed my fifteen minute walk to the station to coincide with a break in the rain. Despite these valiant efforts, the skies opened and the umbrella couldn't save my skirt, legs and shoes from a thorough soaking. It got worse. Out of no respect for my sodden shape, the train experienced technical problems and terminated early, miles from my destination. I then had to navigate a foreign neighbourhood—getting steadily wetter—to locate a money machine, in order to hail and pay for a cab. As Murphy's Law would have it, the driver then took me on an indirect route, which meant that the fare was depressingly equal to the amount I would have paid if I had sensibly taken a cab in the *first* place. Realising this error in judgement and wallowing in self-pity while also being incredibly late, meant that I failed to return Himself's smile when I at-long-last arrived. And from there, the evening spiralled downwards to the depths of dire Dates. With very expensive steak.

Many lessons have been learnt from this lost Date. For this particular Principle – *Arrive 'in Smile'*, my lesson is to prioritise the Date and not the travel discounts. After all, what's a few extra bank notes for a once-in-a-lifetime dinner? And the cab fare would only have been half the cost of the smallest steak. (And yes it was very good steak.) As a side-note, I also remind myself these days to lower my expectations: I had idealised the evening so much, I had set up the Date to fail—there's no way it could live up to how I'd imagined it.

This goes to show that, despite the best-laid plans and well-meaning intentions, matters can conspire against us and we can arrive in a disgruntled state. But we should not allow it to manifest into a discontented Date. We must get a grip on ourselves!

Recovering your Smile

But how do we do this? How could I have switched from a sodden and melancholy state to my best charming and attentive self? Challenging myself, I ask, "If I had *not* been meeting Himself, would I have mustered the energy to strike the pose, smile and be positive, for someone else?"

I must confess that the honest answer is "Yes"! If I were meeting someone for an interview, an important client, respected relative or even a first date, I would have suppressed my self-pity and engaged enthusiastically on arrival, downplaying the bad luck that had befallen me. And here lies an important factor. *A weakness of being in an established relationship is that we can take each other for granted. We freely discard the good and respectful behaviours that we may observe for others.*

Ngaire was increasingly distressed to note that while Anton turned on his charismatic self for dinner guests and drop-in visitors, the very moment the door closed behind them, he would drop back into the grumpy sullen mood that had hung over him for some time (due to his unhappiness at work, Ngaire discovered later). Eventually Ngaire had it out with him: "Why do *I* get the grumpy Anton and everyone else gets the fun Anton?" Anton explained that because he trusted her, he felt he could drop the facade and not have to suppress his mood. Unfortunately he was also taking her tolerance and continued affection for granted.

The purpose of Date Night is a romantic evening for two. We must eliminate any under-appreciation of each other, and entertain each other as deservedly important people. After all, others will come and go: valued clients, close colleagues and even favoured friends. But as a couple you are committed and should be the most cherished people in each other's life. So restrain the angst, value your Date and focus on being *the best that you can.*

However, 'stuff happens'. If you arrive completely wound up by a forced change in plan, the irritating email I mentioned earlier, an unpleasant encounter, a bad journey; if you're far too flustered to strike the right pose straight away, then allow yourself a thirty minute grace period to recover. Assure your mate that you're looking forward to the Date and will be on form very soon, if they won't mind just giving you a moment. Then do whatever you need to do to feel better and restore your spirits. Lock yourself in the loo for a quick self-indulgent sob. Phone a friend to get your sad-faced moan off your chest. Freshen your makeup or splash water on your face. Regulate your breathing until you feel calmer. For some people a stiff gin or a bracing scotch can restore a sense of internal peace and perspective, others of you might prefer a calming cup of chamomile tea. After thirty minutes you must *let it go*, park it for tomorrow, and embrace the Date anew. Otherwise your self-absorption dishonours your partner and the relationship, and obviously compromises the Date.

Actions:

- Arrive in a cheerful mood to set a positive tone for the Date.
- Treat the hours leading up to the Date as important as the Date itself.
- Identify three things you can do to make you feel good before a Date. Then incorporate these activities as part of your pre-Date ritual.
- Establish the most likely things to upset your mood in the pre-Date hours. What can you do to protect yourself from these?
- Think through your journey; avoid any travel tensions through lack of planning.
- Combat stress by imagining you're meeting the most important person you know, and arrive with your usual charm intact.
- Allow yourself thirty minutes to recover if all else fails.

Remember, treat the hours leading up to the Date *as important as the Date itself*. Maybe you hadn't considered this before? This time is about gearing up and cheering up. So whether it's avoiding football scores and rush hour road-rage, or building in tranquil baths and yoga classes, or even sitting down to remind yourself of the other 15 Principles in the Date Night Manifesto, sensibly arrange your time so that you can arrive at your Date in the best of spirits. You've just learned what a difference it'll make!

5. Romance Won't Wait (Don't Be Late)

"The while we keep a man waiting, he reflects on our shortcomings."
— French proverb

Lesson from your early dates: Punctuality promised potential, whereas lateness did not make for greatness.

Would you be late for an important client or guest? No, because showing up on time is a mark of respect. Would you be late for a promising first date? I'd certainly hope not, since you're wanting to start the evening positively, as well as showing yourself in the best possible light. Then why would you be late for the most important person in your life?

The problem is that now you are in an established relationship you can easily fall into less considerate behaviours, and not bothering to be on time is a sign of this. On Date Night, where the idea is to make your partner or spouse feel special and important, it's essential to show your respect and start the evening well.

You'll find this chapter is one of the shortest in the book as punctuality is a fairly clear-cut courtesy. Do I really need to say more than "Just be on time!"?

Yet many people fail to realise the myriad of negative emotions that can be unleashed by poor timekeeping. Let's start with the small stuff: while you are sitting there waiting, you can feel anxious about the practical consequence of lateness on Date arrangements: "How long can I defend the last spare chair from the sharp-elbowed, seat-hungry crowd?", "Will I lose that coveted 8pm table sitting?", "Will they let us into the theatre after the show starts?" And after a while you might start to panic and think, "Should I make alternative plans?" Or you might be more worried about the welfare of the absent party; "Are they lost?", "Has something happened to them?", "Are there problems on the roads?" and so on.

Conversely, if *you* are the latecomer, you could be concerned about the discomfort you might be imposing upon your date, due to 'the wait'. You could also feel nervous about a frosty reception. Take note of the French proverb at the head of this chapter. Alongside your shortcomings, a combination of disappointment and fear of being unloved and disrespected can result in defensiveness; either emotional withdrawal, passive aggressive anger or overt displays of upset. Why invite such unhelpful and purposeless angst? Isn't it safer to simply be on time? In this chapter, we'll discuss ways in which you can be more mindful and encouraging of timekeeping so that you start the Date comfortably in unison.

Punctuality Pitfalls

Just recently, our neighbours Gina and Steve were going out on a Date;

dinner was booked at a local restaurant for 7pm. The clock had raced passed six-thirty then six forty-five without any sign of Steve. Gina was waiting, ready to depart for the restaurant, replete with scarf, coat, keys and clutch. Eventually Steve ambles in at ten past seven, looking perplexed at Gina's ready and now anxious state. He had inadvertently assumed that the restaurant was booked for 8pm, explaining, "You always book tables for eight." Which is true, however, on this occasion they could only get an early table. Gina is the one at fault here, as her lesson is to confirm Steve's understanding of the meeting and evening arrangements. Don't set up your partner to fail on this first step in the Date by assuming, or testing, their understanding of the evening's logistics.

By now you know your mate's punctuality pitfalls, and your own—whether the problem is remembering the time and location, overconfidence with travel logistics, difficulties finding a new venue, or an innate ability to completely lose track of time. So be wise about yourself, and kind to your partner, in order to start the Date in-synch. For example if you have a beauty ritual to rival Madonna's, and like to try on your entire wardrobe to find just the right outfit, then get realistic about the time this requires. (Men, this means you too.) An after work Date, where you have a condensed turn-around time, might not work. Perhaps a late night Date would. But if your partner isn't a natural night owl, making this a less desirable option, you could always do the wardrobe overhaul the day before a Date, and start on your evening face during a coffee break. Being realistic about your own tendencies and then investing effort to avoid a delayed Date sends a clear message about your value of the occasion.

Now for your mate. There are ways that you can help them to be on time, and nagging isn't one of them! I'm talking about genuine acts of kindness. Trevor and Faith are music lovers and like to check out up-and-coming bands on their Date Nights. Faith knows that Trevor is a useless map-reader (and, as per the cliché, this male will not ask for directions!) so his chances of finding a discreet venue in an out-of-the-way location are next to zilch. So rather than be left waiting while he circumnavigates the city, Faith kindly meets him at his work and saves herself the displeasure of sitting alone in a dodgy basement, remote garage or warehouse, or other such aspiring artist venue. At the other end of town Janet knows that Nick likes a power-nap to pep himself for any evening, but being stood up whilst he's banking forty winks just feels wrong; especially on Date Night. So she has gently coached Nick to catch his 'zzzs' on the train home from work or in the cab to the Date venue so it doesn't make him late. (I presume she has also taught him to wake up at his intended stop.)

Unintentionally Late for your Date

But "The traffic accident gridlock! The boss who lobbed some urgent work on me! The sick child! The last minute rescheduled meeting!" What about those unforeseen factors that make you late, even if you have planned ahead? If you know that you're not going to make it on time, then advise your partner that very instant, or at least as early as possible, and arrange to meet at a later time. Because believe me, it's no fun for them—waiting and waiting at the appointed venue at the agreed time without knowing what's keeping you. For some people, there's nothing worse than this wasting of time. So communication is important, and an early message can be liberating. Not only is this being respectful of your partner's time, but it also frees them from the dullness and growing impatience of 'the wait'. Give them advance information and they can choose how to use this extra time. They might want to leave their office later, join an after-work drink with colleagues, take a later train, spend extra time at the shops or pop into the library. Unless you are amongst the rare few who don't possess a mobile phone, there's little excuse for not communicating when you know you are going to be late. And remember to keep your phone charged that day.

Apologise and Make Amends

OK! So you've given the heads up that you're running late. When you do eventually arrive, be sure to say sorry and try to make up for your late arrival. Again this is a mark of respect. It shows that you value your partner's time and that you are genuinely regretful. Would you fail to apologise if you were late to a job interview? By not acknowledging your own misdemeanour and floating in like nothing is amiss, you're demonstrating a certain amount of self-importance or just sheer ignorance about the angst you've created.

My man is pretty much a workaholic—levering Himself out of the office to arrive on time for a Date Night requires a vast amount of resolve on his part. For a number of years I would try to quietly tolerate yet another late arrival, whilst dwelling morosely on how this could only mean that I wasn't his number one. But when Himself does arrive, he lights up the room with his endearing apologies, smile and humour, which never fails to redeem him in my eyes. Once again he is forgiven, and I promptly discard my pessimistic thoughts.

Transforming 'Always Late' into an On-time Date

I'm not the only one. In many, *many* couples there's always one person who is more punctual than the other. (Aha—I can practically see you nodding.) The timing offender is often armed with excuses or defence strategies. One of the most common is the stereotypical cultural excuse "We Italians (or it could be Spanish, Brazilians, Cubans, Kenyans or Jordanians or any nationality other than perhaps Germans or Chinese) are always late". Don't believe them! Regardless of strength of cultural ties, first generation or fortieth, full-blooded or one-sixteenth, this argument is simply an excuse. So if you are in the habit of justifying your lateness based on culture, let me ask you on this: do you arrive at work on time? Do you make trains and flights? Do you manage to catch your favourite television show? You see, if it's important to you, you're *not* late.

The master of defence strategies is lawyer Joan, who is perpetually late for Harry. Cleverly she'll try to reframe her tardiness: "Well I might be late, but I'm not slow! I race in from work and turn myself around in twenty minutes; that's shower, make-up, getting dressed *and* doing my hair". It's true, Joan is quick. But if only she was quicker at leaving the office, she might then have a better chance of being on time for her bloke. Now Joan isn't the only culprit in this story. Harry hasn't been honest with Joan about how he feels when she's late yet again. By not being upfront with Joan, he is allowing the cycle to continue. If he took the time to explain that her being on time would make him feel loved, valued and important, I'm sure Joan would re-prioritise her schedule. But this is more difficult than it sounds. It requires being honest to yourself that you're feeling hurt and under-appreciated. It took me years to let Himself know—and I'm a psychologist! If you do ask your partner to change patterns in behaviour, (such as being aware the time set for the Date arrival is *not* the time to leave the house) remember to positively reward them when they get it right. Yes, like training a puppy. When Joan makes it on time, Harry needs to hearteningly acknowledge the change, without sarcasm either. In this way Joan is more encouraged to keep it up. Positive reinforcement can be a sincere "Thank you for making it on time. I recognise it was a big effort but I want you to know it means a great deal to me". Or if you're more playful, lots of hugs and kisses might not go astray!

A little reward can go a long way. Take this story about a Valentine Date where Himself was more than an hour late. It's true: I sat unaccompanied in a restaurant that was capitalising on February 14th; crammed with couples and heart-shaped balloons, it even proffered pink menus and strawberry chocolates. The timed dinner seating made it obvious that my Date was late, and not that I was early. As the minutes ticked by, the pitying glances from around the room picked up. I felt like I was starring in the dining entertainment—a one person silent show: "Stood up on Valentine Night".

Mindful that this wasn't just another night, nor just another Date Night, but a *Valentine* Date Night, Himself was aware of the gravity of his timing error. He called several times, updating me on his progress as he tried to cross London to the restaurant. To further placate me during these calls, he desperately yet brilliantly suggested that I order the most expensive champagne in the restaurant and that he would pick up the bill—which we usually tended to split. Bubbly is my favourite tipple, as anyone who knows me is aware. So I was delighted to indulge in a pink vintage champagne and was in a welcoming mood by the time Himself turned up.

Learning from this Valentine evening, we have since introduced a standard rule to our Date Night: if you're more than twenty minutes late, then you pay for the bubbly which the awaiting party has freedom to select, order and to start to drink. It's a win-win solution: the person waiting has the reward of choosing the wine, whilst the late party has the certainty of a happy welcome on arrival. This rule has turned into an amusing game: imagine us each racing across London trying to be the first one to the Date Night venue. Black cabs have been sighted, moments apart from each other, speeding down the same street. Cabbies are quickly tipped, and then the fun is to look like you've been waiting for ages—when you haven't—to justify your champagne. The new 'champagne reward rule' has worked—today Himself is rarely late.

Actions:

- Confirm your meet-up arrangements—be sure you're both on the same page. There should be no confusion on Date Night.
- Be realistic about your timekeeping pitfalls. By being wise about yourself, and kind to your partner, you have the best chance of a synchronised Date arrival.
- Advise the other, at your earliest opportunity, if there is any hint that you're running behind schedule. Don't over-promise and under-deliver.
- Be apologetic if you're late, and try to make up for your tardy arrival.
- Gently communicate how you feel, if you find yourself always left waiting, and through this, build a shared understanding.
- Instigate a win-win solution, like the champagne reward for the person left waiting!

So remember: just as being on time is vital to other aspects of your life, punctuality is equally, if not *more* important on Date Night. You are insulating the Date from pointless negative emotions. It shows that you respect your partner and that by being there on the dot, you can't wait to be with them!

PART TWO:
DATE NIGHT DECORUM

6. Hang off Their Every Word

"Love is the feeling of being alone with each other—
yet you're the centre of attention!"
— Unknown

Lesson from your early dates: You paid attention to your date to make them feel great.

Who *hangs off your every word*? Pre-school children? Eager employees? Faithful friends? Social climbers? Paying clients? Dutiful in-laws? Perhaps it's the deli assistant, florist, or some random Facebook Friend. Or sadly just your loyal Labrador. Back on the single-scene it would be a romantically inclined suitor. All of the above desire a token of your affection—whether more trade, time or treats. And this is what you want on your Date: affection from your mate (treats are good too!).

So Date Night is the time to *hang off your partner or spouse's every word*.

This Principle is at the very core of your approach for Date Night and underlies your entire Date Night Decorum. It's all about being uber-attentive.

If you are already fairly confident on the social circuit, now you need to apply your finely honed people skills to your partner. Or maybe you've proven yourself at refining corporate relations? Use these interpersonal skills on refining your closest relationship.

But if you're like the majority of us and are not the 'hostess or host with the most', here are some guidelines to ensure success on your Date Night—which you can even carry over to social entertaining opportunities. (A bonus!)

From the beginning of the Date to the end, you really, really, *really* need to behave attentively. Have I stressed that enough? What this means is making your Date your number one priority and showing affection, whilst prompting conversation and *actively listening*. If this sounds like a 'big ask', guess what? These are simply basic hosting skills. If you've ever entertained houseguests or clients, you may have done all these things (OK, you might want to hold back on being too affectionate with clients) with the aim that the recipient of your attention feels special and is having a good time.

So let's look at attentiveness in the context of Date Night. You've made it through the Manifesto's *Date Night Prep*; you're fully energised and ready for action (Principle 1) assuredly, you've booked a romantic venue (Principle 2), you're suitably attired in finery to impress your date (Principle 3), arrived with a smile and in good spirits (Principle 4) and done your best to show respect by being on time (Principle 5). The stage may be set for a great night, but it's not the time to relax. Absolutely not! Now it's time to up your game. And your success will critically depend on your ability to behave attentively.

The Attentive Arrival

Don't underestimate the opening scene of your Date; it is important to be fully attentive from the start. Take a lesson from another of my ill-fated evenings.

We had arranged to meet for pre-movie drinks at a popular central London bar. It was a dark, wet night and there were problems with public transport but I was determined to get there on time (see Principle 5 – *Romance Won't Wait (Don't Be Late)*). However, I was literally 'running late', frantically weaving between the rush hour crowds and enormous puddles to reach our venue. My relief at arriving in time was short lived—Himself seemed to be enjoying the company of another blonde at the bar. The "Here I am!" smile dropped off my face. Whilst it is perfectly acceptable to engage in conversation with others, blondes included, it's best left until *after* the opening scene. But this doesn't mean we have to avoid contact with anyone apart from the waiter. As you'll learn in Principle 14 – *Keep Your Eyes on the Prize (Your Beloved),* it is possible to make your partner feel like a priority when you're with others.

My man and I are becoming more successful at the attentive arrival, or the opening Date scene. In Dublin, a favourite Date rendez-vous was the Shelbourne Hotel, an ornate historical landmark. Whenever Himself greeted me in their lavish lobby, I liked to imagine we were featuring in our own old Hollywood movie. Whilst our hotel venue might sound overly glamorous, it is really the intentional welcome that is key. My friend Alison, who has just celebrated her thirty-third wedding anniversary, has taught me a thing or two about treating a spouse. Ahead of any special evening she'll stake out the rendez-vous and charm the staff into saving her prime seats and even show them how to mix husband Tim's favourite tipple. Tim arrives feeling like a king, irrespective of whether he's relaxing fireside at a pub with his perfectly poured Guinness, or at a museum cafe, perched on a firm sofa with his Darjeeling tea (and a squeeze of lemon). If you are meeting somewhere before your Date venue, think about how you can make their arrival feel special. Can you save fireside seats, or seating with a view? Maybe a landmark or special surroundings could be put to romantic use.

Captivating Conversation

When first dating, did you ever caution yourself from talking too much? If so, you may have especially reprimanded yourself for raving on about pet subjects. The sports team you follow religiously, real estate prices, office politics, *national* politics, the sex life of the earthworm... don't we all have hobby topics of conversation that are exciting for ourselves but cause others' eyes to glaze over? Early in our relationship, Himself playfully introduced a ban on two topics being discussed in the bedroom: he called them my 'two Ms'—that is, my tendency to talk about my mother, and Myers Briggs (a personality tool that makes me excitable—just not in the between-the-sheets way). Surely you have your own conversational passion-killers? Identify these and aim to avoid them.

On Date Night, you should make an effort to be proactive and initiate conversation that makes the other person feel special. As popular psychology reminds us, asking someone about themselves is a sure way of making friends and influencing people. OK, you may think that after years of being a couple you know everything about each other—work and daily schedules, friends and food dislikes, and so on. But I wouldn't mind betting there are multitudes of thoughts, ideas and reflections that haven't been shared. Sometimes we get in a pattern of not sharing them simply through lack of time, or an assumed lack of interest. Or one (or both) of you may not be a natural chatterbox. So here's where you take the initiative: focus the conversation on your partner, and on getting them talking. Then you can *Hang off Their Every Word* and behold what a difference that makes!

Don't be too superficial. Questions like "How was your day?" or

"How was work?" may sound like meaningless stock questions, the equivalent of a store assistant's "How are you?" a standard greeting to a stranger. So cut to the chase here and ask things that you genuinely want to know. What do you really want to learn about their day?

And before we look at some example questions, take note: if there's a subject you don't particularly want to hear about, then *don't ask about it*, especially if you suspect you will be bored. Boredom is hardly conducive to romance so don't invite it by bringing about a topic that'll make your mind drift. If you find yourself struggling to keep awake, tactfully cause a change in conversation, for example "Before I forget, I've been meaning to ask you about..." Or sideline the conversation with a flirtatious compliment. The suggestive "What can I do to make you feel special tonight?" will most likely reward you for interrupting.

Essentially you need to take ownership of the quality of the discourse and change the conversation if it's not stimulating. Like a good dinner party host, you are responsible for entertainment, including your own. I've outlined below some exploratory-styles of questions to replace the stock standard "How was your day?" With these, try to follow it up with an associated further question (as shown), sometimes it's the second or third prompt which can draw out more interesting information, and hence stimulate a pleasing conversation.

- What was different about today? *followed up by*... Anything else?
- What were you grateful for? Why?
- Who did you appreciate the most today? How can you return your thanks?
- What did you learn this week? How might you apply these lessons?
- If you could replay the day/meeting/event, what would you change? Anything else?
- If today was a film, what would it be called? What genre would it

fit into? Which actors would you cast to star in the key roles? (This can be quite a fun discussion!)

- Why was doing X or seeing Y important to you? Can you say more?

The above examples show how the standard "How was your day?" question can be reworked to provoke a thoughtful response. For more meaningful questions see Principle 10 – *Reveal More* and you'll find intimacy-building dialogue cues throughout the rest of Part Two: Date Night Decorum.

Remember to transfer, to your Date, those 'being attentive' techniques that you've already developed with your friends or colleagues. For instance, you might demonstrate your attentiveness to a client by verbally recalling what they have previously told you, thereby showing that you value what they have to say. Likewise, look for opportunities to remind your partner that you remember insights she or he has shared from other occasions: "Was that like the time you did X?" Socialite Josephine finds herself jotting a list of must-ask-about reminders before a night out with a friend. She even admits as much, as she draws from her clutch the list (sometimes a valiant A4 page, other times a meagre post-it note): "I've been thinking about you and would be disappointed to forget to talk about..." In addition to asking questions, Josephine might have some funny stories that she wants to share, or follow-up thoughts to earlier conversations. On the receiving end it's flattering that she's gone to the trouble to be so mindful. Can you do the same with your partner?

Body Language – Striking the Date Night Pose

If this was a book for first Dates, we would explore courtship gestures which include preening, touching the hair, smoothing clothes and so on. But are such gestures as evident in established relationships? There are mixed views on this. Naturally body language plays a big role in communication.[6] Taking this into account, it seems essential that on a Date Night your body language supports the romantic intent of the evening.

Body language includes how you modulate your voice, as your vocal tone, speed and volume can radically alter how a message is received. Throw facial expressions, physical proximity and gestures into the mix, and the whole package can support *or divert* your romantic objective. Take television newsreaders as an example—they have learnt to deepen their voices and slow down their speech in order to command more attention and inspire confidence. Whilst this is highly staged, recognise that *you* already adjust your style for different environments, whether you're trying to impress a new client, empathise with someone in stress, summon children, or call a trained pet (which is often done in a sing-song style). On Date Night remember to adjust your non-verbal communication accordingly. You might need to remind yourself to smile more, soften the eyes (a phrase I learnt from my yoga teacher) as doing so tends to erase facial tension, or switch off your stern parental voice / clipped office manner for a more open and approachable style.

Being mindful about the non-verbal aspect of your communication is also vital for when you're listening. Actively listening with attention to the speaker's feelings is an essential element of making a person feel special. You are encouraging their conversation by showing interest in what they are saying. My friend Adele says the biggest gift her partner of twenty-five years can give her is to carefully listen to her, and in this way she feels valued and understood, which affirms her deep connection with him. By actively listening, not only are you flattering your partner with undivided attention, but you may discover your partner revealing more about themselves. (See Principle 10 – *Reveal More*.) And that's something you don't want to miss!

If you've ever sat with a counsellor or psychotherapist, you'll notice they are excellent listeners——after all, that's a vital aspect of their position. So take some tips from these people. You will see them giving the occasional head nod in acknowledgement, leaning closer to show interest and keeping steady, but not intense, eye contact to reinforce their engagement. We are all sensitive to eye movement. And you can tell, can't you, when a person you are talking to is only listening with half an ear: their eyes start to wander. Cathy will attest that her ex-husband had a habit of wandering eyes; he would be engaged in conversation with Cathy, yet his eyes would follow other skirts across the room!

What you will rarely see from any counsellor, or practiced active listener, is distracted eye or body movements, crossed arms, leaning back, or fiddling excessively with a pen or piece of paper. In my sessions, I find myself murmuring "aha" with a slight head nod to prompt further disclosure from my clients. Others might say "Can you tell me more?" If you're looking for bonus points with your partner, try summarising in your own words what you've just heard them express. If this seems awkward, then make a comment to acknowledge the feeling he or she has just conveyed: "You seem really energised by this" or "I sense your anxiety". Such feedback articulates that you've really been paying attention to what they've been trying to communicate. You are *Hanging off Their Every Word*.

Physical Proximity — Closeness Counts

On Date Night, be alert to your actual proximity to each other. The aim, after all, is to get intimate! A physical sense of togetherness can subconsciously promote a positive emotional connection. If you sit opposite each other at an oversized table, it may seem more like a business dinner than a Date, being less ideal for intimate conversation —let alone the seductive brushing of ankles. Our neighbours Angela and Charles, a couple of eight years, like to sit side by side, whilst

Himself and I prefer sitting at right-angles. Both positions ensure that we can comfortably focus our attention on the other without having to raise our voices. (For more on romantic venue choices, see Principle 2 – *Book Your Table for Two*.)

Many Dates can be vulnerable to proximity problems. A theatre buff, with the last tickets for a limited run show, found himself waving to his wife from across the balcony. Sarah and Larry, treating themselves at a spa to a lavish couple's massage, were disappointingly separated on arrival: Sarah to the Ladies' wing and Larry to the Men's area, then individually massaged. They were then ushered into the spa's relaxation zones, where they could drift around like ancient Romans, garbed in white robes, sensually draping themselves on loungers and nibbling grapes, along with restorative herbal teas—but even here, the men and women were segregated. You could say this segregation was Caesar-like too, except that open bi-sexuality was common in Roman times, whereas Sarah had been separated from her lover! So you can have a nice time at a spa destination, but as for *Hanging off Their Every Word*? Hard when you're in separate rooms.

Appropriate Affection

My friends wouldn't describe me as an affectionate person. I'm definitely not a 'hugger' and am a somewhat reluctant 'air kisser'. That makes me not exactly the most romantically demonstrative person. However, if you are like me and know your partner is sensitive to physical attention, then you must remember to be affectionate. If it doesn't come easily, train yourself. After all, your partner is the person you want to be more intimate with. Himself and I often walk arm-in-arm or hold hands, but I sometimes need to remind myself to stroke his back and, once seated, to touch his arm. It's the small things that count! At the very least, be open to receiving affection from your partner; there's nothing more off-putting than a rigid iron-board response to a hug, playful squeeze or nestle on the shoulder. Do avoid being over-zealous with public displays of affection though, and behave appropriately for your surroundings. Holding hands at a restaurant is one thing, but sitting on the other's lap is another. That's when you'll hear people muttering "Get a room"!

Actions:

- Focus on making your partner feel like your number one priority.
- Think about how you can make their arrival special.
- Identify your own conversational passion-killers and aim to avoid them!
- Initiate and follow up on conversation. Take responsibility for the quality of the discussion.
- Match your non-verbal communication to the romantic intent of the Date.
- Listen actively, by acknowledging the feeling and content of what's being said.
- Demonstrate appropriate physical proximity and affection.

The ultimate thing to remember is that to *Hang off Their Every Word* is to behave attentively, which involves good hosting and entertaining skills. And luckily there are plenty of places to practise. With friends and family, at work or at home, you'll always find opportunities to initiate meaningful conversation whilst polishing your attentive listening and non-verbal communication. Keep practising—your Date Night will benefit, and so will your significant other.

7. Every Venue Has a Silver Lining

"A restaurant is a fantasy—a kind of living fantasy in which diners are the most important members of the cast."
— Warner LeRoy

Lesson from your early dates: You signalled your warm-heartedness by liking the venue (even if you didn't).

The air conditioning is a fraction too cold, or the people at the next table are louder than they need to be. The waiter is slow, overly attentive or not attentive at all, having served your dish with the sauce you specifically asked to be left off. However bad the situation, steel yourself... and Don't Be Critical!

Being negative is a sure way to directly derail your Date Night. In fact, avoiding negativity deserves a whole Principle to itself, which I'll soon discuss in depth.

Every Venue Has a Silver Lining could be otherwise named 'Being

Positive About The Setting'. It's a subset of the *Negativity No-Nos* — Principle 12, and importantly it sets the tone for the Date. Don't let the 'cloud' of the original saying settle over your Date Night. By expressing appreciation for your environment right at the start, (for instance "This restaurant is so charming" or "These seats are perfect"), says to your partner "I am here to have a nice time" and "I'm going to value this Date". You are reassuring them that you are not about to take the evening, including him or her, for granted. This is a great confidence booster for them and helps them to feel special—a key aspect to romance. From this platform of warm-heartedness you will find other Date Night Principles easier, from Principle 8 — *Toast Your Togetherness* and Principle 9 — *The Etiquette of Flattery* to Principle 13 — *Be a Lover Not a Fighter*.

Essentially, *Every Venue Has a Silver Lining* is your Date etiquette enabler. It paves the way for all kinds of positivity. You'll find it far smoother to go from "I really like the décor" to "You look delicious in that dress". Try moving from "I hate the artwork" to "I like your shirt". Awkward, huh? Being mindful and appreciative about your environment will have you focusing on the good stuff—then it's easy to transfer this thankfulness to your partner and relationship, setting the course for celebration and compliments (Principles 8 and 9). This can be particularly helpful if you're shy or less practised at dishing out praise.

Signal your Warm-Heartedness

Practising *Every Venue Has a Silver Lining* has the added bonus of making you more approachable; naturally it's easier to have an intimate conversation with someone who is pleased with their surroundings. Who wants to whisper endearments to someone who is critical? I have learnt a lot about the attractiveness and value of being positive from spending time with our classy neighbours Angela and Charles (albeit not on our Date Night!). Whether dining or travelling, they consistently reinforce the good aspects of any setting or event. I find that not only are we eager to go out with them, but we also enjoy more meaningful conversations, invariably sharing more personal information about ourselves. Basically, Angela and Charles are warm to be around. This makes them more approachable and we trust them to be receptive to whatever we have to say.

From my story, you can see this Principle is useful in helping with another: Principle 10 – *Reveal More (but No Strip Tease—Yet)*. The ultimate aim of *Every Venue Has a Silver Lining* is not to review the place, but to prime the Date for those more intimate conversations. There's no need to spend the entire Date gushing compliments about the setting; they're of most value at the beginning of a Date or when there's a break in conversation. When you arrive at the venue, as you're getting settled, this is a good time to share an encouraging response to the place. Oops—is your partner missing this opportunity to be positive? Prompt them by enquiring "What do you like most about this place?" Then during the Date, if conversation has stalled or has digressed to unromantic issues such as household decisions (which I will most certainly be addressing later on!), here you can reset the dialogue by expressing appreciation about the venue or event.

Encourage the Organiser's Efforts

Being positive is additionally important if your partner made the arrangements for the Date. Of course, it's respectful and well-mannered to be gracious about someone's efforts and choice of venue. But if you choose to be critical you could curb the organiser's enthusiasm for organising more Date Nights. This is no doubt stating the obvious. Behavioural psychologists also point out that negative reinforcement means that a person is less inclined to repeat an action, whereas positive appreciation will have an encouraging effect.[7]

I'm always exploring new Date Night venues, usually a variety of differing restaurants. Sometimes they're great, often they're far from perfect. Mercifully Himself is a gracious Date and I feel encouraged that my experimentation is valued. These days I don't feel the need to apologise, or cringe with embarrassment at less-than-ideal features. The Principle has had the side benefit of upping my positivity overall!

Just a week ago I organised a Date Night involving a new Jazz bar followed by dinner, and lo and behold, the evening's good intentioned choices soon revealed a series of venue faults. There was the forty-five minutes to get a drink at the bar; yes seriously, *forty-five* minutes—and we were their only guests. The enormous club chairs were so far apart, we needed sign language to talk—and that's without any Jazz. Then the restaurant excused the crucified meat due to the departure of their only chef. Rather than decrying it a debacle, Himself found it all quite amusing—including my alarmed reactions. For that I'm grateful. I'm also even more enchanted—with him, that is!

Unlimited Silver Linings

You'll find this one of the easiest Principles to carry out. There are hundreds of elements that make up a dining or other Date setting, which gives you innumerable opportunity to communicate the many 'silver linings' of the experience. If you're bored at the theatre, don't rip shreds off the tired story lines or the poor accents. Instead, choose to comment on the unusual costuming, creative staging, the thoughtful lighting or the music and so on. And be careful of sarcasm disguised as positivity, such as "Well at least the seats were comfortable".

Chasing Away the 'Cloud'

But to play devil's advocate for a moment, what's so bad about sharing your frustrations? Having a little whinge about the wine? Enjoying a mutual complaint about the garish lighting, the wobbly table, or the pianist's cheesy repertoire? After all you're with someone who knows you well, understands your personality and knows what sets your teeth on edge. Well that's fine and dandy much of the time, but this is Date Night and starting the evening with a negative comment can be off-putting for romance, which ultimately requires you to present yourself as loving and lovable. Negativity can make you appear as neither and can even reduce your attractiveness. Oh dear! And as if that weren't bad enough, it can spark a downward spiral into Bad Date territory. The reality is that most whingers and moaners are not desirable or attractive company. If you've made the effort to dress well (Principle 3) and look your best, why spoil the picture by being a Moaning Minnie or Whinging Wally? Some people might suggest that the sharp-tongued Simon Cowell is sexy, but many may wish to argue that particular point. Best to keep the halo firmly in place and not to swap it for the devil's fork.

And as for the aforementioned downward spiral, let me tell you about another one of Cynthia and Clive's Dates, planned at an esteemed and expensive restaurant, and anticipated with considerable excitement. After being seated, Clive asked to change table, not once but *twice* – the air conditioning being too strong, then the size of the table too large. When, at their third table, he started to complain about the service which was overly attentive, Cynthia confesses to feeling anxious, silently willing the hapless waiter not to return to the table in case Clive barked at him some more. Subsequently, the divine Date at a luxurious restaurant descended into an awkward evening devoid of romance. Cynthia can now make sense of Clive's complaints as his wanting the experience to be perfect. Yet it would have been more successful if he had managed his expectations down or, in the face of cold aircon, just kept his jacket on.

If you are, however, so uncomfortable that you are distracted, then you will need to address the situation to find that silver lining. Any such efforts should be communicated in a warm tone showing a generous attitude. So rather than "I'm so uncomfortable I can't think" or "What were they thinking, putting us under the aircon vent!", try "Honey, I really want to spend the evening focused on you. The aircon's a little distracting, would you mind if we changed tables?" Here you're reinforcing the importance of the evening, and since the comment is affirming rather than negative, you're heading in a good direction.

If you only had 'one chance ever' to date your husband, wife or partner, would you waste any precious moments being negative about the event or venue? Heck no. You would be well-mannered and respectful of each other and the rarity of the occasion. You would signal 'I am not going to take you, or this evening, for granted', by showing some appreciation for your environment. With all your energy focused on your beloved, you'd barely register that your table is too close to the restrooms.

Actions:

- Begin the evening by spending a few moments appreciating your environment.
- Resist expressing any criticism about the venue; behave like a gracious guest.
- Prompt your partner if they aren't taking up the opportunity to be positive about the venue: "What do you most like about this place?"
- Mention your concerns if you truly are uncomfortable, but make sure you use a warm tone. And continue to be affirming about the evening.

Every Venue Has a Silver Lining—being positive about the setting—is a quick win. It's easy to accomplish, it encourages the organiser, and most importantly it communicates warm-heartedness. As mentioned earlier in this chapter, it paves the way for other Date Night Principles such as *Toast Your Togetherness* (Principle 8), *The Etiquette of Flattery* (Principle 9) and *Reveal More* (Principle 10). It creates your fundamental 'up' disposition; in short, it sets you up for a successful Date.

8. Toast Your Togetherness

*"The more connections you and your lover make, not just between
your bodies, but between your minds, your hearts and your souls, the
more you will strengthen the fabric of your relationship, and the more
real moments you will experience together."*
— Barbara De Angelis

Lesson from your early dates: Back then you celebrated the
mere possibility of a relationship. (Now you have something real
to celebrate!)

As a couple, you are a Team—whether it's team 'Tina and Tom' or team
'Gillian and John', or even team 'Justin and Ron'. And like any winning
team, you need to be motivated and enthused. Focusing on what *is*, as
opposed to what *isn't,* can have an empowering effect on your
relationship. Date Night is the perfect time to sit back and celebrate
your joint strengths and achievements, and look to a positive future.

Business psychologists have found that by articulating a team's strengths and successes, team members become more heartened to relate to each other in a genuine way.[8] A vision too can be incredibly motivating; sharing hopes for the future can really boost a team's commitment levels, inspiring more effort and enthusiasm. You know what's coming. Yes, we are going to apply proven team techniques to your relationship and Date.

Team Strengths

There is an Asian expression: the crown of a tent only gets closer to heaven when you lengthen the tallest pole. In other words, working on weaknesses (the shortest poles) serves in achieving mediocrity, but not in achieving greatness. Work on the strengths as well, and your relationship could be great.

A couple's strengths can arise from complementary differences and combined similarities. What are your team's strengths?

Peter, a New Zealander living in London, has been married to Layla, from Syria, for over a decade. He recognises that their cross-cultural marriage opens doors to diverse worlds, which is stimulating and full of constant surprise. Peter suggests that a key strength is their generosity of spirit and strong family values. When Peter's mum was recuperating after surgery, Layla travelled across the world with their newborn to aid his mother's recovery. (Three flights and thirty hours with a squawking bub in economy class—now that's dedication.) Likewise, when they bought a holiday house in Syria, Peter made sure it was large enough for Layla's extensive family. I hope that they take time to recognise and celebrate their considerable strengths.

If you find it difficult to identify your united strengths, ask some friends to simply describe you as a couple. Their responses will invariably reveal your strong points. For example, most people would describe Kelly and Casper, married five years, as an adventure oriented couple who constantly seek new experiences. These are clearly their united strengths; because of their union Casper has become a confident snowboarder and Kelly has competed in wacky car rallies which involves driving decorated vehicles across several countries. Another team, Alison and Tim, are known as fun for their parties, plentiful liquor cabinet and fondness for late nights. Perhaps your team has a reputation for a relaxed cheerfulness, mutual enjoyment of books and movies, or for being nature-loving hikers with the best tips on vegetarian cooking. Valuing what makes you special as a couple, your unique strengths, will forge closeness and intimacy. Just raising awareness of these strengths can spur you to do more with them!

Team Achievements

"Haven't we done well!"

"Look where we've come from."

Recognising joint achievements is your mutual pat on the back. Articulate your successes during your Date Night; it fosters enthusiasm, promotes good spirits and generates the warm fuzzies. Academic psychologists who explore the factors that contribute to happiness speak enthusiastically of such 'savouring' and its role in our psychological well-being.[9] They encourage sharing memories, self-congratulations and counting blessings as meaningful ways to savour.

What are some of the things you might savour? Begin by thinking about your mutual accomplishments and blessings to date. Perhaps an ornate garden, inspiring friends, amusing children. Frederica and Roger rejoice in the fact that their adult sons often seek to join them for weekends and holidays. This is down to Frederica's great hospitality and the couple's combined ability to spark thought-provoking conversation, which could be seen as a team strength. Together Frederica and Roger have successfully created an alluring environment which blends comfort and warmth with stimulating and intellectual company, keeping their sons returning for more.

Reflect on what you both hoped and wished for and then realised. It could be long-term aspirations: raising children, settling close to family or retiring early. It could be more immediate goals like getting to know the neighbours, going on safari, learning more about wine, or selling your property successfully without paying an agent. Whether long-established and meaningful, or short-term and relatively superficial, all aspirations offer opportunity for savouring a team accomplishment. After several exhausting years spent renovating a derelict Victorian house, Himself and I dreamed of modern apartment living. Upon moving to Dublin we rented an apartment with restful views over Malahide Estuary. The ebb and flow of the estuary tide was a dramatic shift from the rotation of construction skips. On Date Night we were often found recognising this achievement, our liberation from dust, builders and DIY; even after eighteen months we still felt like we were on vacation (thanks to the shorter 'to do' lists, dependable plumbing and the blissful underfloor heating). We celebrated the joys of the change and the fewer bills to pay!

So go ahead and recognise yourselves as a team—think about what you've achieved *together* that might not have otherwise been possible. Take a moment too to recognise how it has contributed to your growth and development as two individuals. My female friends Lauren and Janet are both very much in love with their husbands of twenty-plus years. I have heard them express enormous appreciation for their relationships in how these provided opportunities they would not have otherwise had. Janet the amateur actress can be heard saying if it weren't for Simon, she wouldn't have travelled as much: "I'm far too scared to have chosen to live abroad". Lauren, a school teacher, will say, "I love the fact that we both seek change—we have lived such an interesting life." Such genuine sentiments would be well suited for a Date Night. Now in case you were finding these to sound like an anniversary-type conversation, well indeed they do. But why reserve such powerful sentiments to a once-a-year occasion?

Team Vision

If voicing your relationship's achievements sounds like an anniversary toast, sharing your team vision will sound like a New Year toast. This is when you express your hopes, wishes and dreams for yourselves as a couple. And *couple* is the operative word here. Any personal aspirations to spend a future alone should probably not be included in Date Night!

Some couples do discuss wishes, hopes and dreams quite naturally—and for some, it may even be a fundamental part of their relationship. Nigel and Susan are a fine example of this. Married for twenty-two years, they are on track for early retirement, their long-term goal and joint vision since they were dating in college. Sacrifices have been made along the way, indulgent vacations and extravagant gifts forfeited. Susan recalls the regular moves, with their children high-schooled in three countries, as Nigel sought his next step on the career ladder. It's this resolute commitment to their vision that is a hallmark of their relationship, and a testament to its success.

If, as you read this, you feel confused or perplexed about what your vision might be, or you haven't really thought about it, quite likely there is something that you're working towards—you just haven't put it into words yet. Completing the following phrases might help you to articulate your thoughts:

- I hope for...
- I wish for...
- My dream is that...

So when do you share these thoughts? There's no need to worry about randomly voicing your wishes, hopes and dreams. Such expressions make for excellent dinner Date toasts. Here again, it distinguishes a Date Night from another meal out. Himself and I can be found raising our glasses to toast our vision during many a dinner Date: with the first drink of the evening, then again when the food arrives.

Alternatively, discovering your vision might deserve a fuller conversation. You could begin with this question: where could your team strengths and joint values take you together? See where this leads. It is likely to be an exciting and thought-provoking dialogue.

Actions:

- Identify and share your combined strengths. How can you use them in the future?
- Count your blessings as a couple and congratulate yourselves on your achievements.
- Ask yourself - what have you achieved through the relationship that wouldn't have been otherwise possible?
- Toast your future!
- Be careful not to overdo it. Sharing one or two positive memories can make the evening meaningful and thought-provoking, but too many might sound clichéd and devalue your genuine sentiment.

Toasting your relationship is an obvious activity for a romantic evening for two. This Principle's focus is on you as a team, allowing your strengths and achievements to bolster your bond and reinvigorate relationship satisfaction. And sharing your vision, wishes, hopes and dreams helps to consolidate your commitment.

9. The Etiquette of Flattery

"Love not expressed is not love at all."
— Himself

Lesson from your early dates: You let them know what you liked about them.

Do you sometimes feel taken for granted? Well you are. Sorry. Not all of the time, but much of the time. Think about it—does it feel like certain parts of you, maybe your most endearing qualities or selfless efforts, have become unappreciated and invisible? Regrettably, many an affair, or marital failure, has started because the otherwise committed man or woman simply found that appreciation elsewhere.[10]

We are all guilty of taking our partners for granted. But with a bit of focused effort, which is easy on Date Night, you can protect yourselves and the relationship from the dangers of an appreciation deficit. You can remind yourself of the many things you treasure about your mate, and reassure them that you are mindful of this.

Taking each other for granted is a problem in most familiar relationships, whether it's your partner, mother, sister or best friend. As an established couple, the frequent support you give each other becomes, over time, an expectation in the relationship. In the beginning you might have slaved to perfect your homemade pasta, and it may well have received its deserved praise. But now you've had many opportunities to serve up your pasta creations, is that special recognition less forthcoming? Likewise there are many things your spouse does for you, that you used to recognise and value, and now you don't even think about anymore. Go on, admit it.

I have. I once delighted in Himself's attentive and precise hanging of my art pieces, but now I fully expect that he will display my creative endeavours, and am likely to get narky if he appears lax on that front. Too often it's only when a companion is not there, and we miss their care-giving or helpfulness, that we have a stark reminder of how much we take for granted and what we really appreciate.

Give Thanks for What you Would Miss

I was recently reminded of the perils of taking the other for granted: we were attending a large dinner event, and on our table there were four couples and Eric—the only unaccompanied man. Eric, in his sixties, came across as a successful and confident businessman. Over the course of the evening, I uncovered—aided by his thirsty consumption of wine—that his wife of thirty-seven years had left him. Even now, two years after her departure, he was struggling to cope; he confided in us that he's thankful to be still working. I couldn't help feeling sorry for Eric, and yet I also couldn't help supposing (rightly or wrongly) that he must have taken his wife for granted. It is true, absence can make the heart grow fonder. But really, remembering to express fondness and thanks can help to ward off unwelcome departures. It's an act that also makes the heart swell.

"Appreciation can make a day—even change a life. Your willingness to put it into words is all that is necessary." – Margaret Cousins.

Besides, research[11] shows that meaningful expressions of gratitude can have an immediate and prolonged impact on happiness—for the person doing the expressing. So now there's no excuse. You should be fully motivated to convey genuine thanks. After all, it's a feel-good act for both of you.

There are many things you can be thankful for, from the little matters of daily life, to the deep-seated personal attributes. I'm forever appreciative (and guilty of not always expressing this) of Himself's quick wit and challenging intellect. Yet when he's away on business, which can be a couple of weeks at a time, I am keenly reminded of more subtle aspects of his personality that I might fail to acknowledge. I miss his ability to engage with the world: he's the one who does the introducing and conversation opening when we are out. I miss his evident enjoyment of my culinary experimentation with food or restaurant choices. I must admit that when by myself, I'm not as motivated to cook or set foot in unfamiliar restaurants. He brings out my creativity and helps with my social confidence.

Now it's your turn. What endearing personal qualities would you miss if he or she weren't there? Would it be their relaxed disposition and astute insights? Their *joie de vivre* and playfulness? Their sensitivity to others and centred spirituality? What do you really appreciate about the other person in your life? As I did with my culinary expression, reflect on what is it that they do which brings out the best in you.

Gratitude Reaps Rewards

It's equally important to appreciate the little things. You might feel relatively blasé about chores or small acts of kindness such as cleaning the bathroom, helping with the DIY, managing the school-run or bringing you a coffee—but these are, after all, the building blocks that make up your everyday life. You'll be pleased to hear this: studies show that expressing gratitude for these everyday gestures can be a powerful mechanism for couple growth and perhaps even a booster shot for romantic relationships.[12] Now there's a quick win! Why? Because proclaimed gratitude has a reciprocity effect (encouraging an exchange of nice acts) which serves to sustain healthier relationships.

So through gratitude you are encouraging mutual kindness, and by giving specific thanks and praise you are reinforcing desired behaviours. It's a sure 'two for the price of one'. As proven in behavioural psychology,[13] where certain behaviour is acknowledged positively, it is reinforced and more likely to be repeated.

Learning via Appreciation

If you were a fly on my wall, you'd hear me intentionally thanking Himself, giving positive reinforcement for any act that I would love to have him repeat. On Date Night I might be heard saying "Thanks for making it on time. It makes me feel like I'm your number one." (Remember my issue with his tardiness from Principle 5 – *Romance Won't Wait (Don't Be Late)?*) Throw in a winning smile, playful squeeze, hug or kiss to supercharge the positive reinforcement! What behaviours do you value and want to encourage more of?

See how giving thanks and showing appreciation is a form of feedback, and also a valuable learning opportunity? The gratitude you show each other communicates what you like. Armed with this information, you might choose to do things differently. For example, Angus delighted in an elegant fresh floral arrangement that Milly designed for their hallway console table, replacing a couple of long-standing potted orchids. Now Milly feels licensed to embrace her inner florist and contort blooms into all sorts of strange, and hopefully elegant, positions for his continued delight.

Note this: when you show gratitude, not only are you *not* taking your significant other for granted, you are saying that you're happy that you're together. It can make both the receiver and expresser happy, it reinforces that you value each other and strengthens the good stuff: kind acts and desired behaviours.

Have you observed how some people are quite gruff about saying "thanks" or don't seem to say it at all? You might be naturally good at expressing thanks or gratitude, but many folks aren't. Like me, you might have grateful thoughts but fail to articulate them. Or you might simply take the good things that the other does for granted. Either way, Date Night's focus on you and your relationship provides a perfect opportunity to practise being verbally thankful, to communicate how much you value each other, and to learn more about what each other likes and enjoys.

Give Genuine Compliments

Why give compliments? Hey, why not! It's an expression of your admiration, respect and value for each other. Don't we all love a compliment! I was once told by a 'man about town' that "flattery is the *art* of making another person feel good". This maxim should definitely apply to the person you've chosen to spend a good chunk of your life with.

OK, so with that thought in mind, you can safely assume that *any* compliment is OK—yes? Actually, no. Overused compliments can be associated with social niceties and clichés that have little meaning. The more cynical persons amongst us will only respond to a genuine accolade. I'm a sceptic. If presented with an admiring comment I will turn it over in my mind to examine its credentials: is it valid, or is this person just trying to schmooze? The "you look lovely" compliment will sometimes work. *But* when I've battled gale force winds and now resemble a scarecrow, you've got to be joking. The 'compliment' will appear a trite obligatory statement and so obviously not reality that it could even be deemed sarcasm. If it fails the authenticity test, I become irritated and suspicious of their motives—can't they think of anything better to say? Or worse still, what do they really want! Authentic expressions of admiration or praise only, please. My advice? Avoid the potential for irritation and be sincere with your compliments.

When giving a compliment, maximise the bang for your buck by making it especially meaningful to the person you're giving it to. Meaningful accolades are memorable. What compliments do you remember? I recall Himself saying he was inspired by my discipline to write every day. Himself inspired by me! That made me feel great. I remember him admiring my braveness to go swimming in the sea despite being 'blind as a bat'. Wow—I had never given that a second thought, having always been horridly near-sighted, but I guess it is brave given what might be lurking beyond the waves. See how these person-specific compliments can really make your loved one feel good and achieve the art of flattery motto from above. You'll find that meaningful compliments are tailored to the receiver and require some thought; they're not saccharine sentiments that can be passed out like toffees to just anyone.

Gracious Acceptance of Recognition

Now, receiving compliments can be just as much of an art. Particularly if they make you self-conscious or uncomfortable. You might not be used to receiving praise, or you're suspicious like me, or going through a period where your confidence is at a low. Whatever your situation, be gracious, assume good intent and in lieu of a better response, simply smile and say "Thank you". Don't screech, "Are you blind?!" or "What? This old thing?" Challenging a compliment (see Principle 13 – *Be a Lover Not a Fighter*) is definitely not permitted on Date Night. If the compliment confuses you, you are however permitted to warmly invite more information.

On a recent Date Night Himself said to me that he loved my shoes. What, those truly old things? I had owned them for at least five years and wore them regularly, so he had certainly taken his time to notice them! Instead of sulking about his lack of attention to my wardrobe, I decided to cheekily enquire what he liked so much about them. He responded that he loved the way they matched my outfit to perfection. Since I'm normally adverse to dressing overly 'matchy-matchy', his added words made sense and made his compliment authentic. Oh— then there was the positive comment about my new perfume: I must have looked bemused because I wasn't wearing any. I still smiled, assuming his good intent, and said, "Thank you." After some thought I put two and two together, recalling that I had swapped my usual hairspray to Elnett, which has its own distinctive scent!

A few well-meaning compliments, shared here and there on Date night, shows that you are paying attention and that, in itself, is flattering.

Whilst Principle 8 – *Toast Your Togetherness* – is all about appreciating your union or team, this Principle – *The Etiquette of Flattery* – is focused on showing your respect and admiration of each other as *individuals*. Both Principles reinforce your delight in having your spouse or partner as part of your life, fully priming you for a romantic evening.

You have much to be grateful for. Use Date Night as an opportunity to show your appreciation and remember, you'll get the most mileage out of sincere and person-specific compliments.

Actions:

- Share your appreciation for the big and small things they do for you. What would you miss if they weren't there?
- See their expressions of gratitude as an opportunity to learn more about what they appreciate.
- Give genuine and meaningful compliments. What do you admire about your partner?
- Receive all compliments graciously.
- Try not to overdo it. Too much can get cheesy.

With this last action, you can again learn from my mistake. I mentioned in Principle 6 – *Hang off Their Every Word,* that I was not particularly demonstrative person. Likewise, giving compliments is not my strong suit, probably because of my natural suspicion of them. So after scoring ourselves against the 16 Principles (see page 201 for evaluating your Date Night) my performance on *The Etiquette of Flattery* was my weakest area—it needed work. The next Date Night, reminding myself to do better, I dished out my first compliment, which had an immediate positive impact. Bolstered by Himself's beaming smile, I went on and on, spewing forth praise and admiration—until Himself's smile turned to an expression of suspicion. And I knew what *that* felt like.

So let's repeat that again: don't overdo it!

10. Reveal More
(but No Strip Tease—Yet)

"We are not the same persons this year as last; nor are those we love"
— W. Somerset Maugham

Lesson from your early dates: You decided what you might reveal to your date, and what you'd hold back.

Do you know your partner's inner world—that is, their values, life goals and aspirations? You might pride yourself that you'd do well on a green-card test. You know the type: "What's their preferred toothpaste?" "What side of the bed do they sleep on?" "What's their music of choice?" This is the easy stuff. It's factual, directly observable and doesn't rely on interpretation. But the inner workings of the mind is the true seat of what makes us tick.

Does your significant other know what keeps *you* awake at night, *your* deepest regrets and most cherished memories?

Scientific studies of three thousand relationships over thirty years have discovered that couples feel closer, and are better able to weather stress, when they really understand each other's world.[14] The research proposes that we should devote more cognitive space,[15] and time for this pursuit, so that we continually enrich our knowledge of our husband, wife or partner. It's simply about remaining interested. History's romantic adventurers would seem to agree with the academics of today: Casanova is quoted as saying "Love is three quarters curiosity". What could you uncover on your next Date Night?

Attempting to discover a person's internal self is like an old-time explorer seeking new lands; there are simply no maps, guides or GPS, only persistence, care and attention to detail. Early settlers would document their findings and note changes in the environment, or surprises in the terrain, as an aid for others and for their own safe return passage. Now you might be thinking 'We've been together for ten/twenty/thirty years, I rightly know the terrain!' But like any territory nothing stays the same. Your childhood neighbourhood is not the same. Where that fabulous strawberry patch roamed is now a car park; the old Scout Hall is now overshadowed by a residential block; the park has been improved with a delightful cafe. So don't rest on false assurance—the person that you faithfully took time to understand at the beginning of the relationship is not necessarily holding the exact same perspectives, thoughts and aspirations.

If you're quite sure you know what makes them tick, ask yourself: how did you come to think this? Is your information 'straight from the horse's mouth', or have you made your own assumptions? And how *current* is your assessment? You could be correct; you could also be quite wrong.

Some marital advice advocates keeping a record of your discoveries about your husband or wife. In this, you could document aspects of your spouse's internal world, from simple likes and dislikes, to their personal goals, hopes and dreams. Recently married Annie enthusiastically

114

explained to me that she keeps a notebook dedicated to her husband where she references any findings, from his pleasure at the smell of jasmine, to bigger issues like his remarking that he found peace from his volunteer work with disadvantaged youths. Some months later, when he revealed an aspiration to give more back to society, she was able to encourage him to leave his lucrative decorating job and apply for a permanent position with youth services. Annie's demonstration of understanding and support is a result of her keen interest and mindfulness of her husband and this means that he feels listened to and valued. It's a good forward step on their marital journey. If you, like Annie, are inclined to keep records, that's perfectly fine. But please, please don't bring out your notebook on Date Night!

So check. How *current* is your understanding of your loved one? Have you each kept up to date with how the other might have changed? People's life goals, hopes and aspirations can evolve (but values less so). As we mature, we brush up against the reality of life—or we have it smack us rudely in the face—and this can trigger an alteration to our views, especially as we are forced to recognise our limitations. So you're not going to be a world-class swimmer after all. Writing a prize-winning novel while running a household with kids isn't exactly happening. So gaining that top finance position *does* come with a cost: working seven days, spending most evenings away from family life. It's no surprise that our goals may go through a transition.

According to Cognitive Behavioural Psychology, our inner world is made up of numerous mental models; each model is a product of our past and present circumstances. A change in any number of factors can bring about a shift in one or more models. Bob, a colleague, once viewed success as retiring early—it was one of his life aspirations. Notching up overtime was his way to fatten up his pension fund. Now approaching fifty, Bob has encountered a number of discontented, bored or frustrated early retirees. While also observing many stimulated, youthful-hearted employees in their seventies (including Tim McCain who ran for US President), he has shifted his framework, or mental model. Bob now actively seeks a more fulfilled and balanced working life, rather than early retirement. He leaves the office before six o'clock and has picked up new hobbies including learning Spanish and dancing the Tango. He seems more satisfied. Bob's baffled wife did speculate about the presence of a Latino mistress!

It's natural that we continue to grow and develop as individuals.[16] In fact it would almost be impossible *not* to adjust one's outlook, views or life philosophy over time.

You might be more tolerant than you once were, or perhaps you no longer suffer fools gladly. You might've modified your life aspirations in line with current reality, like Bob did. You might find joy in activities or foods that were once foreign to you. You might have discovered that aspirations have failed to bring their expected rewards. Like with me, the prospect of a good book and comfortable bed might have become far more appealing than partying until dawn. You might even be a reformed criminal who has found God. We go through life constantly adjusting our views and mental models. I remember my Grandmother being vocally anti-Russian, as a result of living through the Cold War, then transforming this entrenched position after visiting Moscow and St Petersburg in the Soviet Union of the 1980s. On this trip she had been overwhelmed by the kindness of her welcome and the undeserved respect and assistance that she received by the local Soviets. Life's experiences and surprises can render a change in our perspectives.

Understanding More About Your Date

Date Night is an ideal time for conversations that help you explore, test, validate or build upon your understanding of your mate's world.

Just one or two investigative questions are enough to spark a deep and meaningful conversation. Please do not attempt *all* these questions in one evening! You don't want your significant other to feel they are being interrogated.

Starter questions to keep up your sleeve, for learning more about
your partner:

- I recall you aspiring to... Has this changed?
- Who currently inspires you, and why?
- What do you think has changed for you, since living in ... /
  working for ... / having the children / since the children have left,
  etc. Do you think others have noticed a change?
- Who is your current role model? Has your role model changed
  over the past few years? Why do you think that is?
- If you could change one thing, what would it be?
- How would you like to be remembered? Why is it important to you?
- What achievement are you most proud of? Why? What
  achievements would others *assume* you to be most proud of?
- What's on your bucket list? What would you most like to do in your
  life?
- I was puzzled when you chose to do ... Can you help me to
  understand what was going on for you at that time? (A good one
  for Bob's wife!)
- What gifts have you received over the years that you most value? Why?
- What are you looking forward to over the next month / quarter /
  year? Why?

Alison kindly agreed to try out a couple of these questions on a Date
Weekend with her husband Tim. A weekend meant they'd have lots of
time together; a good opportunity, Alison figured, to explore more
meaningful conversation. Personally, I was intrigued to test my
theory—that even after thirty-plus years together she would learn
something new. On her return from the Date Weekend, Alison reported
that she was delighted with the exercise. Not only did she learn a lot,
it was intimate: Tim enjoyed the conversation and she felt deeply

connected to him. She added that she didn't need to force or contrive opportunities for the questions, but that they easily arose during the conversation. For example, when Tim mentioned his relief at successfully completing the management of a large safety audit, she casually asked, "Do you think you've changed since taking on this management role?" He replied no, he didn't think so. As coached, Alison then enquired, "Do you think others have seen a change?" and this is where he offered new information and shared that one of his staff, who was studying for an MBA, had asked whether he could use Tim as an example of a senior executive with accomplished management skills. Alison was impressed, proud and pleased for Tim. Yet she wasn't surprised that Tim hadn't brought it up before—as she puts it, "he's not the bragging type". The conversation with Tim didn't end there—he built on the topic and asked if she had seen a change in him. And onward their meaningful conversation flourished.

You will see from questions listed above that I advocate exploratory enquiries—the 'why' questions. The purpose of these is to keep the conversation open and moving along. Most importantly, they should help to bring about new revelations. Let's say that your mate has answered "Who currently inspires you?" with a succinct "Gordon Ramsey". The follow-up "Why?" question will then explore whether your partner is inspired by Chef Ramsey's irreverent use of the English language; or his ability to traverse from football to cooking to television; or perhaps it's his good physical shape and media attention; or even his robust family life. The various explanations to any of the 'why?' questions can initiate an even deeper conversation and voila!—an insight into your partner's world.

Make sure you adopt a warm and tender tone when asking the question, and importantly follow-up by listening actively. In this way, you are likely to communicate genuine care and interest (See Principle 6 – *Hang off Their Every Word* for tips on engaged body language) and receive a thoughtful and expressive response.

But what if he or she resists opening up to your questions? To lighten up the conversation, try approaching from a more casual direction. Begin by revealing something about yourself first. And be sensitive to the timing of your *Reveal More* investigation—later in your Date when you're both relaxed might be more appropriate than within the first hour.

Sharing your Internal World

On *my* Date Nights, I'm far more comfortable asking the questions and exploring Himself's mindset, than I am talking about *my* inner world. It could be an occupational hazard for psychologists. But if you're like me and less comfortable expressing your deeper self, it could be due to any number of reasons. Maybe you've fallen into a habit of not sharing the important shifts in your internal world. Life can be hectic—are you both so busy that you seldom converse on the small questions of everyday life? Well, no wonder it's harder to converse on what matters inside. Or maybe you are embarrassed or think your musings will be scoffed at; that your partner will not understand or appreciate their significance, or might even find them boring! It could be that, when growing-up, a parent or sibling trivialised your thoughts. Perhaps you've rationalised that your reflections are simply too private and you need to work through them before discussing.

On the other hand, you could be withholding personal insights as a form of withdrawal from the relationship. "Unless he/she bothers to ask, why should I bother telling them?" Some people can enjoy a sense of power by being secretive. Oh dear, so many excuses! And they all point to a disconnection and a lack of trust.

Kim was surprised by a revelation of her partner's, during the course of a dinner party. "Why did you never tell me you did some time in the navy?" she asked the environmentalist later. Jacob's answer "You never asked" is defensive and not a terribly good excuse. The truth though about Jacob, described by Kim as a 'dark horse', is that he was an only child, then 'something of a loner' as a teen and twenty-something. He was simply unused to opening up to others. Privately, Kim is highly amused by his maritime revelation, it does cast a more rounded light on the man in her life. Kim desperately wants to have some fun and switch his stereo alarm from Sanskrit chants to the Village People's 'In the Navy'. But she's careful not to turn him off from opening up further. What more might there be to discover?

Date Night is all about re-establishing the romance for committed couples, which requires a sense of connection and trust. So take a risk, open up and share something new and meaningful about yourself.

You Need Not be Asked

Don't sit back like Jacob, waiting for a direct question about your internal world. During your Date there are numerous opportunities where you can offer a nugget of insight to the inner you. For example, you can start the conversation with...

- I've been reflecting on...
- I've been surprised at my reaction to... I wonder if it's a response to...
- I've been realising how important ... is to me. It offers me... and ...
- I was inspired by meeting/seeing... As a result I'd love to try...
- I've been especially enjoying...
- (or more seriously) I want to share something important to me...

On Date Night you might want to share an insight, vision or dream, or the meaning you make of these. Take a troubled sleep of mine: in my dream I was panicking about being unprepared for exams. I didn't have much time and they were going to be complicated. Upon waking, I was relieved to discover I currently lead an exam-free existence. For the next few days, I walked around in a state of bliss, relishing that my exam days were over. Sharing this with Himself, we embarked on a discussion of the many years that I spent studying and his persistent support for me during that time. So how about talking about the dream feelings *you* experience, and whether you can associate those feelings with current life issues.

If sharing dreams sounds a bit wacky, or maybe your dreams feel too wacky for sharing, then this next approach will work for you. Your significant other has seen you grow as a person over the years, and should be able to offer valuable insights from their own observations and their point of view about what makes you tick. Therapists and counsellors call it 'holding up the mirror' – when you reflect back your observations on someone. This can spark interesting and rewarding conversations. Letting anyone hold up a mirror to you requires trust, confidence and respect, which is perfect for Date Night—it's a great acknowledgement to the value of your relationship. Try these conversation starters:

- How do you think I've changed over the past few years?
- What do you think I'll miss if we move from here? Or if ... changed?
- What directions do you see me moving in the future?

Now remember: receive their views graciously. Whatever you do, *don't jump up and down and get defensive*. If what they say is not what you want to hear, you can ask clarifying questions to really understand their perspective. Date Night isn't the place for contradicting or correcting each other; it's the venue for acknowledging each other.

Actions

- Use Date Night conversation to enhance your understanding of each other's internal world.
- Make enquires *gently*. It's not an interview or a test!
- Hold back some questions for another Date. Just one or two questions can spark a deep satisfying conversation.
- Be prepared to reveal something new and meaningful about yourself.
- Demonstrate your respect; trust and let them 'hold up the mirror'.
- Treat new information graciously.

So on Date Night, when you're settled into your surroundings, quietly instigate conversations that help you explore or build upon your understanding of your partner's world. And be ready to share yourself. Revealing more about yourselves will help you to feel closer as a couple. You will have a clearer insight into what makes your partner tick, and they will discover something meaningful to you. From thought-provoking dreams to evolving social perspectives, new personal goals or life aspirations, the intimacy gained through such topics is perfect for Date Night.

11. Wanted: Good Sense of Humour

"For me, compatibility is a sense of humour; being able to laugh together – that is very important."
— Felicity Kendal

Lesson from your early dates: Laughter on the first Date was a good omen for a second Date.

Wait a minute—did I say humour? Is such a Principle appropriate in the Manifesto, and doesn't it contradict the serious and meaningful sentiments expressed in the previous Principles?

The short answer is No. Laughter, grinning, smiling and other symptoms of happiness will bolster your good spirits, charge your energy levels and reinforce your confidence, putting you in the mood for love. In this chapter, I'll also give you the long answer: how humour can help reframe challenging life events that might otherwise distract from your romantic objective. And finally, how humour offers the perfect recovery for Date Night disasters, when things don't go to plan.

Smiling Makes you Approachable

Cast your mind back to being on the singles scene. I wouldn't mind betting that at some stage, you were captivated by the charms of an amusing man/funny female, more so than by someone who was purely handsome. See how humour entertains, makes you smile and simply makes you feel good. There's something quite flirtatious about a person's pointed attempts to make you laugh. Yet you really should invite their attention—laugh at yourself, initiate the fun, smile! Don't underestimate the power of a smile. I spoke to a serial charmer who confided that he'd never approach a woman who wasn't smiling. At least then, he told me, even if she's not interested, she's still going to rebuff him nicely. And to return to the present, we should note that using smiles and humour is as powerful in an *established* relationship as it is in an early relationship, in making yourself approachable and attractive.

Making your Partner Laugh is an Expression of Love

You'll often hear couples say that a key reason they're together is because their mate makes them laugh. According to Love Lab research—yes there is such a place[17]—long established, highly contented couples have two behaviours in common: a shared sense of humour and frequent expressions of positive sentiment. Sharing exactly the same humour is not always guaranteed though. Humour is essentially a person-centred perspective on what you find amusing; it's been socialised from your earliest days. You might not laugh at their slapstick humour or longwinded jokes, but you might find their dry wit amusing, clever and insightful. So while you couldn't tell a joke to save yourself, you do share an appreciation of the humorous side of life.

I love it when Himself makes me chuckle. He has a keen sense of humour and can impressively turn a sulk into a smile with a single funny remark. Yet on the scale of comedy skills I would score myself a zero; I can never recall a complete joke and my attempts at wit tend to produce confused looks rather than giggles. But to my surprise Himself finds me funny. It took me a while to work out how he could possibly find me even vaguely amusing. Is he surprised that I stay upright in spite of my perpetual clumsiness? With observation, I found him most amused by my ability to laugh at myself; my comical take on an incident (the many blonde moments). I also noticed that when we're engaged in decision-making or serious discussion, my dry offering of an outrageous idea will bring a grin to his face. So learn from this; whether it's subtle or obvious, look for where your humour overlaps, note the root of laughter, and bring it to Date Night. In this positive way, you're recognising and reinvigorating a hallmark of your chemistry. You're emphasising a quality that is unique to your coupledom.

Humour is not always easy, by the way. It requires thoughtfulness and observation to make someone laugh. This attentiveness can be incredibly flattering and is often seen as an expression of love. Sometimes in an established relationship we can get lazy and fail to make the effort that we once would. Think about who you focus on making laugh—your children, close friends, colleagues, or classmates? Challenge yourself to prioritise your partner's laughter.

Italian-born Stefano doesn't 'get' the English 'black humour' that has his Australian partner Lara splitting her sides. Yet Lara has cottoned onto a certain taste in comedy movies that they both share, and has come to instinctively know what Stefano will find amusing. An early movie Date sees them come out beaming and buoyant, primed for partner-focused drinks and charged by each other's good mood and giggles.

Humour can Reframe Difficult Events

During difficult times, humour can allow couples to strengthen their alliance and sustain morale. Himself and I spent a number of years renovating our dilapidated house, which often meant sleeping in some rough, dusty and cold conditions. During a particularly harsh winter the builders unexpectedly disappeared to warmer climates, leaving our house bitterly cold without a kitchen and external wall. On Date Night, we would focus on the funny side—from the concrete dust embellishment on our smart suits to the ridiculous dust masks and heavy coats needed if we wished to watch television.

Life is full of difficult moments (see also Principle 12 – *Negativity No-nos*). Losing a job or anxiously beginning a new job; dealing with health issues, sad news, and incidents like that which happened to Tom and Max, who were burgled while sleeping. Upon waking and hearing intruders, Max, to Tom's horror, went straight down the stairs to challenge them! Fortunately the burglars had scarpered before he made it down the two flights. The intrusion of privacy and loss of items was unsettling and upsetting. Yet, a few days later on Date Night they could be found joking that Max's nudity had frightened the intruders anyway, or chuckling at their absent-mindedness—the foolishness of leaving valuables under bright lights near the front door. "We might as well have invited them in!"

Whatever your frustrations and discomfort, look for the funny side. Even under the most trying conditions, humour can be used to reframe events and situations to release the emotional burden. That tiresome incident can become a future Date Night (or dinner party) anecdote!

Humour as Recovery for Date Night Disasters

Date Night, like any high-octane event, is prone to mishap, disappointment and derailment from its romantic intent. Humour does wonderful things: dispelling angst, evaporating frustration, keeping people going when they're ready to quit. A striking example was when, a few days before a Date, I suffered an allergic reaction which caused my face to swell up like a balloon, with my eyes being enveloped by their lids. The Doctor advised it would take several days for my face to return to normal, during which time we had a Date Night already scheduled. Not surprisingly I felt particularly unattractive, self-conscious, and quite sorry for myself. Rather than indulge my self-pity, Himself fostered a light playful tone, affectionately calling me his pretty pumpkin face. Amused, and relieved, I quickly forgot about my allergy and surprisingly found myself having a romantic time. My self-pity could have easily derailed our Date Night, but thank goodness for Himself. Good intentioned humour is a powerful tool that helps to keep perspective and boost morale.

On Date Night we can find ourselves troubled for a host of reasons. Being ready to use and receive humour suggests a lightening of heart, recognition of good will, and an attempt to not get fixated on details. And laughter is such a 'feel-good' hit!

Marking their tenth year anniversary, Clive presented Cynthia with a card, assumed to be an Anniversary card, but no, it was a Bon Voyage card! Cynthia chose to see the funny side of this, explaining that she could easily picture Clive, moments before leaving the office, rifling through his stationery box, and determining that Bon Voyage was better than Get Well Soon or With Sympathy. Next to the inscribed Bon Voyage he had thoughtfully penned "to our next ten years journey together". The anniversary evening was a romantic hit. Could you imagine what may have happened if she had elected to get upset instead?

So if you or your partner have forgotten an important Date-related task, are frustrated with the journey, disappointed with the day, bogged down by domestic details (see the Principles in Part Three: Date Night Vitamins), or have fallen prey to distraction, don't make it a big deal. Use a little humour to forgive the situation and reposition the evening back onto its romantic track. Imagine now that you've arrived at a Date to greet your mate who is wound-up and distracted by a day of bad luck. Now visualise him/her instead amused at the day for its comedy of errors. See the difference? Humour can liberate you, and your partner, from angst!

Humour's Connection with Revealing more about Yourself

By not taking yourself too seriously and showing your ability to laugh at yourself, you send a message that you're open and relaxed. If you appear comfortable, you'll find yourself and your partner revealing more about yourselves. When in social groups, I keenly observe conversation rituals, and have noticed there seems to be a magic combination of humour and people being open to sharing information about themselves (which in itself can help to fast track relationships). I found myself at a formal dinner party where the stifled conversation of eight virtual strangers was broken when the most impossibly beautiful woman shared a hysterical story about her young son's fascination with swearing. In this way she was dispelling an illusion of perfection, implying that she is in fact down-to-earth and somewhat struggling with motherhood. Her revelation was followed by a host of funny stories that were entertaining and also revealing. I believe that using vaguely self-deprecating humour sends a signal of trust, which others latch onto and acknowledge through their own self-disclosure.

Humour Zones to Watch Out For

Overuse or misuse of humour can seriously undermine the poignancy of the evening. Be careful to use good intentioned humour. Partner directed sarcasm, for example, may not be at all helpful to the romantic intent of the evening. Some people who are uncomfortable with intimacy and/or the Date Night idea might even use humour as a resistance or defence strategy. If you find that humour is frequently employed at the expense of Principle 10 – *Reveal More*, go slowly. Consult page 203 in the Date Night Accessories section for my strategies specific to Date Night resistant partners.

Actions

- Smile! It will make you more attractive and approachable.
- Identify your shared sense of humour and bring it to Date Night.
- Reframe a difficult situation through humour.
- Use humour to diffuse any Date Night disasters.
- Watch out for humour being used as a defence mechanism.

By bringing to Date Night your shared sense of humour, you are reinforcing your unique connection: a blueprint to your coupledom. Your smiles and laughter express pleasure, bolster confidence and good spirits, charging the atmosphere for romance. By enlisting humour you are also triggering light-heartedness and choosing to see the upside of life. In this way, you can bring down defences, put aside current difficulties and make yourselves more approachable to each other. Enjoy!

Part Three:
Date Night Vitamins

12. Negativity No-Nos

"If you want to be loved, be lovable."
— Ovid

Lesson from your early dates: It was difficult to feel romantic when your date was being negative.

Did Casanova catastrophise? Was Don Juan defensive? Was Guinevere glum and resentful around Lancelot? I don't think so. Our romantic heroes and archetypes resisted the many expressions of negativity. There's no charm in fault-finding, nit-picking or moodiness in the romance stakes. So heed this warning—such behaviours will have a deteriorating effect on your Date Night.

The first of our Date Night Vitamins, *Negativity No-Nos,* acts like an aphrodisiac (and spares you the expense of oysters or truffles). It is a fundamental Principle of the Manifesto. You'll have noticed so far a strong focus on *positive* sentiments in many of the other Principles, from

7 – *Every Venue Has a Silver Lining,* and 8 – *Toast Your Togetherness*, through to 9 – *The Etiquette of Flattery* and 11 – *Wanted: Good Sense of Humour.* So why does negativity need its own chapter? Because being negative can directly derail Date Night, sabotaging any seductive ambitions, so you must learn how *not to do it.*

It's hard work contending with someone who is complaining, moody or upset. You're unlikely to be having a nice time, let alone a romantic time. Even just one or two negative sentiments have the potential to escalate the Date into a darker zone, where you are focusing on what isn't right, instead of what is. Worse still is vocally finding fault with your partner, pointing out what they've missed and what they do wrong. Ouch! Undermining one's husband, wife or partner is bound to result in defensiveness, slamming the door on sharing and intimacy. A romantic evening relies on celebrating the relationship and showing appreciation for each other; belittling each other should not come anywhere near it. When Date Nights are routinely spoiled by dwelling on what isn't right, as opposed to what is, you're missing the point—and I bet, missing out on generating real romance!

In this chapter we will touch on some of the sources of negativity that can crop up on Date Night, from issues originating outside of the Date to disappointments resulting from the Date. Are you cringing as you read this? Are you... guilty? Take heart—this Date Night Vitamin offers strategies for lightening your outlook, and managing your own and your partner's negativity, to rescue the romance of the Date.

A Heavy Heart

The heart can be heavy for many reasons. You might be harbouring resentments or disappointments, or dealing with difficulties such as unemployment, health setbacks or family dramas. You might not be dealing well with demands such as a change of job, completing renovations or children changing schools. Whatever the cause of your stress, it's important not to let it ruin the romantic intent on Date Night. This might sound harsh, unsympathetic, even selfish when your worries are about other people—but they need to be put aside for a few hours. Unless you nurture each other, you might not have each other. There are countless stories, for example, about the many marriages that fail to survive the emotional, physical and often financial trauma of repeated IVF treatment. It's been noted that parents of terminally ill children are also prone to high divorce rates.[18] When burdens are great, you can take your focus off each other and risk a broken relationship. Remember Maeve and Connor from Principle 1, who managed a romantic weekend away – leaving their chronically ill six-month old with family? They permitted themselves a lightening of the heart, a hiatus from their load, so that they could enjoy each other, reconnect and invest in their relationship. Who could call them selfish for wanting to strengthen their bond of parenthood?

Having a Negative Disposition

Some individuals have a disposition towards negative emotion; naturally pessimistic, their cup is always 'half empty'. Some people are 'drama queens', prone to catastrophising and making a mountain out of every mole-hill. Yet others tend to be moody, neurotic and anxious. OK, so you might not be incessantly down-beat, but don't we all have moments where we are quick to criticise or are just feeling put out? Such behaviour makes romance difficult. Shorna, for example, is a beautiful long-legged blonde who has achieved esteemed professional success. Divorced three years ago, Shorna is keen to enter a new relationship— yet few men are interested. Surprised, I explored further: it seemed that they found her too critical and moody. She'll sulk or challenge the restaurant manager if the best table is not available for her. If the food takes a fraction longer than anticipated, she'll complain and demand free wine. You would need to be resilient, like-minded, or in serious lust to contend with her unrelenting criticisms and stroppiness.

Even research shows that negative types are harder to be around.[19] You don't say. With this in mind, and whether you are slightly or highly predisposed to bad moods, no doubt you've learnt to curb them, to be respectful of others and the occasion. When you're going to a school reunion or a fundraiser, surely you avoid angsting all over the place! If you're hosting a party, I'll bet you're making cheery conversation to make guests feel welcome.[20] So put the same moderation of feelings into practice when you're out on your Date. Value your partner, focus on the romantic objective and don't backslide into negativity.

Ingrained Patterns of Expressing Negativity

Of course, it's actually tempting to share your negativity with your partner! Most couples will have established a pattern where they can offload their woes and irritations: we can all find it comforting, complaining to someone who knows us well. Let off steam about today's traffic frustration, have a massive moan about your mother, whinge about the state of the nation, or cry on their shoulder about office politics. You're just being yourself, after all. Couples regularly store up gripes to share with each other—many don't even realise that they're doing it. Like Anton in Principle 4, subconsciously you figure your husband, wife or partner is a safer forum than colleagues, family and friends who might take it personally, draw conclusions, or simply see you as badly behaved. Well guess what? If you're capable of suppressing bitterness or whining in the presence of others, then you're capable of holding back the flood gates on Date Night. Be yourself by all means—be the *best* version of yourself.

Partner-Directed Negativity

The most damaging kind of negativity on Date Night would be fault-finding with your partner. Destructive sentiments towards your wife, husband or mate can discourage—nay extinguish—any chance of romance. If you have a bad habit of directing negative comments towards the person you're supposed to love, it could be only a matter of time before it erodes the strength and health of your relationship. Research on couples that have many years together, and continue to be happy, indicates that they normally express twenty positive sentiments to one negative sentiment. [21] Their ability to cultivate and sustain a culture of appreciation is seen as a key factor to their successful relationships. (See Principle 9 – *The Etiquette of Flattery* on appreciating each other.)

Date Night Disappointments

Here's another Date Night danger: falling victim to high hopes, then expressing disappointment that the evening hasn't entirely gone to plan. For me, this is a major watch point. I'm a serious romantic who can get a little too fixated on perfection, but when I do this, I'm setting up the Date to fail. When the wind causes my groomed hair-do to become a 'hair-don't', when there are no seats at the bar, Himself is taking a work call, or we have found ourselves digressing into domestic issues, I admit that often I can't help showing my disappointment. Not that I *say* much—I start to radiate a 'mood'. OK, I sulk! It's rather pathetic and terribly unromantic. So these days I'm trying harder to lower my expectations, allow for mishaps and untimely circumstances, and to not judge the evening as a failure too early.

And speaking of that, beware the early negative judgement. I was talking to Beth, who has recently instated a regular Date Night with her husband of thirty-six years. They had just been on their first of such Dates, and she is already disheartened at its lack of success. Beth recounted that the joy of going to the city's most acclaimed and expensive restaurant was extinguished when she found it empty. Beth and Bobby were unsettled by the lack of fellow diners and what started as commenting on the empty tables, led to nit-picking about the menu and prices, bemoaning its poor location and then being hyper-critical about the food when it arrived. This Date may have united them as budding restaurant critics, but it failed on its romantic objectives. Now if Beth and Bobby had employed the *Negativity No-Nos*, in conjunction with Principle 7 – *Every Venue Has a Silver Lining,* and Principle 11 – *Wanted: Good Sense of Humour*, they could have pretended the restaurant was open 'just for them', and enjoyed a sense of assumed privilege. You see? There are many ways you can turn a negative to your advantage to make an evening special.

On Date Night, it's important to be mindful of the *impact* of being negative and how this can quickly derail the Date. Protect the Date by keeping the Date Night Manifesto and its positive intentions top of mind. By recalling Principles like *Arrive 'in Smile', Hang off Their Every Word, Toast Your Togetherness* and *The Etiquette of Flattery,* you'll ward off any tendency to be down-beat, disheartened or disappointed. In avoiding pessimism— the aim of *Negativity No-No*—you are allowing a lightening of the heart. Hooray! Now you can lower your defences, put aside unhelpful habits and pave the way for an intimate connection. Permitting a lightening of heart is essential to Principle 11 –*Wanted: Good Sense of Humour*, and you'll find this smile enhancer works wonders here. Just *how* is illustrated next.

Managing your own Negativity

Lightening your heart means *not* taking your irritations and woes along to Date Night. Following the Date Night Manifesto is about taking responsibility for being in a positive mood. (See also Principle 4 — *Arrive 'in Smile'*.) So if this means preceding your Date with a call to a trusted friend for a soothing chat, or doing some exercise to calm your nerves and release tension, then respect the importance of Date Night and make time to do it. Off-load the annoyance about that awful customer or excessive bill— the only baggage you want to take is your handbag (or man-bag!).

Lightening your heart also means being *realistic* about your hopes for the evening. For me the Date Night Manifesto score sheet on page 201 helps to set real expectations. I remind myself that it's impossible to get top marks in all dating departments, but if I improve my performance on one Principle, that's a good result. Actually, dating for the committed couple shouldn't have a black and white outcome; it's a journey, a path of togetherness. So I'm mindful not to judge a problematic evening too early, but to be ready to remedy the romance. If I find my own negativity rising, I try to focus on my Date Night Decorum (the all-positive Principles 6-11).

A key aspect to lightening the heart is *kindness*. Good grace, good intention, and excusing your own and your partner's insensitivities, imperfections, misjudged slights or general faux-pas. Helen tells me of a birthday when Ralph surprised her with a treat to a seafood restaurant, forgetting her blatant dislike of fish. She was horrified at his oversight and, sulking, insisted that they dine elsewhere. On reflection, Helen wished she had stopped to see his good intent—it was after all the most famous restaurant in the city, he really did want the best for her. And like all international seafood venues it was bound to offer alternatives to fish and crustaceans. Or as she put it, "It could have opened my eyes to the taste of perfectly cooked fish."

Don't be Drawn into a 'Downer'

Be mindful that a single negative expression permits others to be negative.

Before you know it, you can easily find yourselves skating that downward spiral. It's the dreaded contagion effect – where negative emotional expression spreads.[22] When your partner complains, it's your job to focus on the positive. Point out what *is* working well or remind them of something great happening in their life.

Don't be Defensive

If you're at the receiving end of a negative barb, it's tempting to snap back. But don't! It's time to adopt a different approach; bringing out your sense of humour to diffuse the comment (see Principle 11 – *Wanted: Good Sense of Humour*). Or try reframing the comment to put it in line with the romantic intent of the evening.

To explain how this can work, here's my own story of a quick recovery during an at-home dinner Date. I had gone to a lot of trouble to leave work early in order to shop and prepare Himself's favourite dish. I lit the candles, put on relaxing jazz, and painstakingly transformed myself from cook to attractive dinner date. Himself came home and the first thing he said after silently appraising the dining room is, "Did you forget to heat the plates?" Disappointed, my first defensive thought was, "I will never cook for this ungrateful man again." But I didn't give any sign of this reaction. Instead I leaned against him and cooed: "I know what you wanted to say. You wanted to say 'thanks for coming home early, cooking my favourite supper and looking so lovely.'" He smiled, relieved, and said, "Yes, that's what I meant to say." So, as I did here, when a defensive reaction is rising in you, remind yourself to diffuse it. Forgive your partner's misdemeanour and you'll sidestep a spiral of negativity. It can be hard, but restraint can really save an evening.

You know, life can too easily contain multiple sources of disappointment. To deal with these, whether they stem from the Date

Night itself, or from outside your relationship, I encourage you to lighten your heart – if only for the night. By doing so, with *Negativity No-Nos* you are making room for the positive, choosing to have a good time, and creating the space for romance. Lightening your heart relies on assuming the good intent, a generous spirit and not being too idealistic about the Date. Your partner, husband or wife will find you less self-absorbed, more approachable and easier to please. So let's lighten up.

Actions:

- Discard any negative thoughts before you go out. Remember Principle 4 and plan to *Arrive 'in Smile'*.
- Find another forum for your woes. Date Night shouldn't be it!
- Moderate your hopes for Date Night and don't set expectations too high – and you will not be disappointed.
- Forgive a Date Night misdemeanour and look instead for good intent.
- Counteract a single negative statement with a number of positive expressions to shift and strengthen the evening into a better tone.
- Focus on the all-positive Date Night Decorum Principles: *Every Venue Has a Silver Lining… Toast Your Togetherness… The Etiquette of Flattery* and *Wanted: Good Sense of Humour.*

Combine all of the above and you are priming yourself to be both *charmed* and *charming.* I assure you there is nothing more attractive. You'll find yourself as lovable as any romantic hero – from Aphrodite to Grace Kelly or even James Bond. I task you to embrace the aphrodisiac effect of this Date Night Vitamin.

13. Be a Lover Not a Fighter

"Love is a game that two can play and both win."
— Eva Gabor

Lesson from your early dates: You were on conflict alert watching for signs of sensitivity. An argumentative date would rarely get a second opportunity.

Conflict is a normal part of a relationship. It's *expected* even. Who hasn't had a falling out now and then? If the pair of you can successfully manage your conflict, congratulations on the maturity and emotional strength of your relationship. However, Date Night is not a test of this— its objective is romance. If the outcome turns out not to be peaceful, the Date Night's intent is likely to be compromised.

The bond between partners involves the highest level of attachment, love and loyalty. With this intense positive emotion can also come the 'flipside'—a corresponding negative side. Remember the Love Lab? They've researched this too! Their research indicates that for conflict to *not* compromise the relationship dynamic, you'd need— within a pithy discussion—a ratio of *five positive* to *one negative* sentiments.[23] In other words, you would need to be fairly confident of a continued warm disposition and open-minded reception before you'd navigate into stormy waters. Given the risks, I'd simply *avoid* arguments on Date Night. Save your conflict resolution skills for another time.

I remember one ill-fated Date Night whereby we were seated in a stunning restaurant, and had already argued on the way there. Himself opened the evening with a sarcastic toast: "To our briefest Date Night ever." I promptly fulfilled the prophecy by getting up and walking out. Whilst Himself was certainly at fault for his antagonism, my response was hardly mature. Today, I'd like to think I could muster a response that would not destroy the Date Night. I could sweetly reply: "It sounds like we have some issues to discuss, I think we might be best focusing on them at the weekend." Perhaps a playful: "I shall prove you wrong, kind sir, with a toast to enjoying the wine and happy thoughts." Or a confused but caring: "I don't think you meant to toast to that, shall we start again?" Just like the 'lighten your heart' strategies presented in Principle 12 – *Negativity No-Nos,* you are *choosing* to save the Date Night and forgive misdemeanours!

Forgive and Forget (if only for Date Night)

When pocketing your wallet or preparing your handbag, be sure to pack some *forgiveness.* Here I am thinking of Anna and Glen. Of their twenty-six years of marriage, there seems to be two distinct periods: the fourteen years before the affair and the twelve years after the affair. Whilst it's a testament to their commitment to the relationship and family that they are still together, Anna seems to be continuously seeking opportunities to punish Glen. Clearly still hurting after many years, she often uses special occasions, anniversaries, or Date Nights as high-octane opportunities to flaunt her moral high ground and remind him of his misconduct. We're all imperfectly human, and like Anna and Glen, we're all vulnerable to mistakes. You will too easily remember times when your mate let you down. It doesn't need to be an affair; maybe they failed to express support when a loved one died, or they missed the children's end of year play. For Cynthia it's the once in a lifetime holiday that she preciously planned, which Clive then cancelled due to pressing work commitments. On Date Night you need to be generous spirited, forgive and forget about it (even if for just the night). Are you yourself entirely without fault?

Avoid Conflict Zones

But wait—what's bugging you? Something is niggling away and you can't let it rest. If you're puzzled by your wife's extensive business trips, or your partner's increase in drinking, exercise caution. *Don't* bring it up on Date Night! Deal with it in advance of the Date, or park it until a day or two later, and focus on having a nice time. If you just can't let it go and fear it might be blurted out on Date Night, deal with it as soon as possible.

An occasional issue that arises on a Date Night is that one of you, *encouraged* by the heightened sense of togetherness, closeness and intimacy, then tries to address or confront an area of difference. Hey, it might work for the political play of international diplomatic relations but not for a distinctly romantic agenda! You could sabotage the evening, especially if the differences are entrenched and emotionally volatile.

Couples who stay happily together commonly report not always agreeing on the big issues. They have learnt to not let them get in the way, because even the best intentions to *resolve* differences could result in rubbing salt into a wound. Sheila and Mark, for example, have fourteen and sixteen-year-old sons. Mark is regularly chastising Sheila for overly mothering the boys, spoiling them with her undivided attention: ferrying them to and from school, cleaning their rooms, making their beds, even ironing their socks. Mark would rather they were less indulged and more independent, suggesting that they can certainly make their own way to school and they should assist with some household chores. Sheila will snap back, "They'll be gone before I know it." Yet at some level Sheila is eager for Mark's endorsement of her parenting style, so looks for opportunities where she might be able to elicit his approval. Unfortunately her attempts at recognition merely highlight a fundamental difference in values, fostering further frustration in Mark. It's no surprise that on Date Night, their parenting differences is a no-go area for Sheila and Mark.

What are your no-go zones? Do you clash over politics or religion? Are finances a sore subject? Do retirement plans create conflict? The advantage of being in an established relationship is that you're familiar with these 'bones of contention'. When you're on the singles dating scene or first getting to know someone, whilst you're doing your utmost to avoid contention, you don't know where the danger areas lie, and like a hidden landmine, you could set one off. A joke that your friends found funny could spark a radically different reaction, a faux-pas that might extinguish the romantic fuse. I remember, when single many years ago, going on a Date with an IT professional. As we walked through busy Covent Garden, he made a joke about some plus-sized women. I was appalled, and not knowing how to respond, I took the opportunity, in a crowded pub, to permanently escape his bigoted views—slipping out a side door (easier than climbing out a toilet window!) while he made his way to the bar.

Being the Lover (not the Fighter)

We all know how to provoke our partner: you know the location of their

Achilles' heel and what's sure to get a bite. Relationship sparring is a game of tit-for-tat until someone is trumped. This is a game of no winners: you might have won the round, but you've lost the chance of romance on this occasion. (We're not talking about 'make-up sex'— that's another kettle of fish!) To stay true to your romantic aim, enter Date Night with a generous forgiving spirit and use warmth or humour to dispel any disruptive behaviour. Mike Moore, an international speaker in the field of humour and stress management, advises people to use self-deprecating humour to lighten things up. He remembers one evening having an argument with his wife, Carol. In the heat of the moment she said something hurtful. Surprised, Mike looked at her and said, "Carol, when you say things like that you stoop to my level." She started to laugh and so did he. It wasn't long before things were back to normal. In Principle 11 — *Wanted: Good Sense of Humour*, I talk about the importance of adopting a warm playful tone, and using humour to deflect potential conflict. You can see this in action from Mike's example.

How well would you diffuse antagonism on Date Night? Consider how you normally respond when your button has been pushed. A little defensively, huh? Think how you might de-escalate this to a more appropriate Date Night reaction, given that you want to feel connected, intimate and aligned to each other. Just as I've mentally replayed my restaurant walk-out episode, it's worthwhile imagining such scenarios or replaying past experiences, and considering what could you have done differently to preserve the Date. Could you find the funny side? Or take the Love Lab's advice, and counteract the negative sentiment by warmly expressing a number of positive sentiments (remember the 5:1 positive to negative ratio). The warmth of your response is important! Note how vocal conflict is often led by the tone of voice. Sharp, staccato utterances or loud shrills will see a defensive reaction, generating an argument or moody silences whereas soft and gentle tones will ease the tension.

Let's say the Date is underway but an argument has arisen. You've missed an early opportunity to stifle conflict, you've been unable to bite your tongue, and now you sense that you're both spiralling into a worsening negative state. Here's what you do—apply the brakes by bringing attention to it. Saying "I think we're in a downward cycle" or "My goodness we've let this tit-for-tat get out of control" can cause you both to pause and reflect. With this heightened awareness, you can both act to de-escalate the situation. Remember, it's always good to follow up by expressing something positive, like "We have come a long way together" and "We have a lot to celebrate" or "I love to see you smile". Restraint is a wonderful thing, by the way. In practising restraint, you choose *not* to blurt out that retort that will hurt your partner or escalate an argument. If you confess yourself to be too impulsive, or you simply 'can't help yourself' when you bite back, try to be self-aware and exercise self-control.[24] Choose to *Be a Lover, Not a Fighter!*

Destroying Date Nights

What about the spoilsports? Given the significance of Date Night as a romantic evening, some people might harness this power and intentionally ruin the evening by raising contentious issues. We all have those emotion-inducing 'red rag to a bull' areas. I've already mentioned that as an established couple you'd have quickly learnt what is likely to get a rise from your partner, as they would have for you. Where no amount of constructive conversation, calm reasoning or logical argument is going to shift your or their perspective, it's fruitless to go here, and particularly destructive on Date Night.

If you find *yourself* regularly sabotaging Date Night, try and work out the root of this. Could it be a response to feeling undervalued in the relationship? Could it point to an insecurity—perhaps a lack of confidence in your partner's commitment? Maybe a deeply held, unresolved anger for past misdemeanours? These issues are best faced with a qualified relationship counsellor or through individual therapy. Whatever you do, don't create a legacy of repetitively destroyed romantic nights. This will cause future Dates to be faced with apprehension, caution and defence, and you'll have to invest in some serious damage control to restore the relationship's faith in Dates.

As Date Night has romantic intent, it relies on intimate conversation to foster a sense of connection. Going at each other's throats obviously spells Date Night disaster. But also raising sensitive issues, even mildly prodding at danger areas, is a recipe for misalignment. Why open a can of worms?

Actions:

- Identify the no-go areas—topics to be avoided. Remember, "don't mention the war".
- Raise sensitive subjects that are bugging you well in advance of a Date or set aside an alternative time to address the issue.
- Mentally rehearse deflecting or de-escalating a contentious issue so that you don't let it ruin your Date Night. Perfect a warm response— soft voice, positive sentiments or a little self-deprecating humour.
- Defuse 'tit-for-tat' by naming it: "I think we're in a downward spiral— we've gone off track." And then express something positive.
- Consult a relationship counsellor if your Date Night is regularly used to vent conflict, there are likely to be deeper issues at play.

Remember it takes two to tango; fuelling conflict will find you dancing date-less (figuratively, *and* possibly literally). Rather than rise to the bait, you can *choose to diffuse*, and try to save the Date. *Be a Lover Not a Fighter* and practise responding with humour and warm positive sentiments to put the Date back on track.

14. Keep Your Eyes on the Prize (Your Beloved)

*"Put your heart, mind, and soul into even your smallest acts.
This is the secret of success."*
— Swami Sivananda

Lesson from your early dates: You guarded the evening from scene-stealers and other distractions!

Date Night involves intimacy and closeness between *two* persons not four, six, or an entire football team. Intriguing strangers, friends you bump into, the presence of children, the phone calls from colleagues; if you let them, other people can easily steal the show. In today's world of smartphones, tablet computers and other online devices with their terribly distracting 'apps', we are undoubtedly more vulnerable to interruption than ever before.

Remember how in Principle 6 – *Hang off Their Every Word*, I outlined good behaviours which demonstrate your focus on your mate? From the attentive arrival, proactive conversation and active listening, to body language and physical proximity, there's only room for the two of you. This Principle – *Keep Your Eyes on the Prize (Your Beloved)* is about being mindful of scene stealers—those disruptive influences which can upset Date Night attentiveness. And we are all prone to these.

Responsibilities like work or elder/childcare can certainly arise and distract us from Date Night's romantic objective. But the most dangerous of all Date Night distractions are things that are *usually* welcome. Of all the Date Night Vitamins, this one can be the hardest to swallow. Things like greeting old friends, phone calls from distant children, or being excited by the event—perhaps a musical or sporting occasion—where your Date is taking place. Of course these are all wonderful and welcome things… but be aware that they will shift intimacy to the back-burner as your priority moves away from your partner.

Others versus your Beloved

Everyone knows the saying "Two's company, three's a crowd"—hence on Date Night we don't set out to seek the company of others. Yet sometimes it just happens. One of my dearest friends, Adele, confirmed how potentially romantic evenings can be ruined by the inclusion of too many people. There's nothing kinky in this situation! Her partner Jerry has a larger-than-life personality and likes a good time, and his idea of a good time normally involves a large group of people. So much so, that Jerry loves to engage in conversation with strangers—at the bar, in the subway, at the restaurant. It's not unusual for their planned evening for two to end with drinks for four, six or more. Adele told me that she sometimes just gives up on the romantic evening, leaves

Jerry to party into the small hours, and goes home alone.

While Jerry is an extremely sociable character, all of us are prone to the distraction of others. Himself and I were visiting a French seaside town, and happily earmarked a local seafood restaurant as a Date Night venue. The tables were small, the environment intimate and I had visions of us savouring a sensual evening eating *moules mariniere* with our fingers while enjoying a live jazz quartet. As it happened we were in for a surprise – the place was filled with tables of French women. *Quel distraction!* For Himself, as a hot-blooded male, of course? Actually, it was I who succumbed. The unexpected female camaraderie was simply too tempting. It began when the neighbouring table of three women confided that the Brazilian male waiter was responsible for drawing in the large numbers of females. I felt immediately compelled to also admire the aforementioned waiter; I'm pretty sure I only commented that his English was good, but Himself insists I was eyeing him up and down! (Purely out of curiosity, of course.) Needless to say, this is hardly good behaviour for a Date Night, with our *moules mariniere* for two soon becoming razor clams and sea snails amongst five. This sounds like it was a fun evening, but in fact I spent the evening feeling sheepish that I had allowed Date Night to be hijacked. Himself confirmed afterwards that he felt like a spare part. So watch out for potential hijacks—Date Night is about making each other feel special and *not* like mere accessories.

Don't worry, I'm not saying you can't talk to strangers. I *am* saying put your Date first and keep them the centre of your attention. If you were responsible for entertaining an esteemed client, friend or guest, you might engage in chat with others, but continue to demonstrate that client/friend/guest is important to you. You might even compliment them or note their accomplishments in front of the others. If I am with my friend Jane, I'd be the first to reference her recent book publication. And I am always delighted to hear Himself praise *me* in public, for instance "I can't take any credit—I learnt it from my wife". (For more on compliments, see Principle 9 – *The Etiquette of Flattery*.)

People can distract you without even *being* there, thanks to the delights of technology. While communicating with others by SMS or email may be marginally more acceptable than a live phone call, you are still essentially ignoring your present company and choosing to prioritise another. In this way, you are *not* behaving attentively or making your mate feel important.

Ever observed one person enjoying a hearty phone call, while their companion looks wistfully around the room or examines the cutlery in great detail? Yep, modern technology is a definite distraction to romantic intent! If you have to take a call, minimise its disruption: keep it brief and keep focused on your partner. For example, you can mention them to the caller: "I'm here with John enjoying a wonderful evening." Don't turn away, smile at them while talking to your caller, or hold their hand. These efforts clearly signal who your priority is.

No doubt you've witnessed couples out on Dates who are *both* on their phones. Why are they out at all? After nineteen years of marriage, Cheryl and Simon can sit together at a restaurant and spend the entire time consumed, not with each other, but with their separate texts and calls to friends and family. Cheryl confessed that when they're feeling romantic, they'll text each other from across the table! At least that's *some* attention. Remember that regardless of medium, behaving attentively on Date Night is about your partner being *numero uno*. And that certainly isn't demonstrated by hogging half an hour on the phone to your sister, or interrupting dinner by texting your best friend back because you "simply have to". Needless to say, playing with your phone apps or checking the latest updates is the height of rudeness on Date Night.

Be Present with your Beloved

Exposing yourself to regular disruptions can spoil your ability to be really thoughtful about your partner, yourself and the relationship. Without this mindfulness, are you really able to charm your loved one? Will you still be in the mood for romance?

My friend Susan realised what a passion-killer her husband's Blackberry was. Nigel's texting and emailing was so constant, he may as well have had his Blackberry surgically implanted; it was with him while eating breakfast, barbecuing dinner, taking a bath, resting in bed. Susan arranged a vacation, without their teenagers, to a golf resort near Palm Springs. On arrival, Nigel was disconcerted to discover that in this desert spot he had no internet connectivity. Without the perpetual distraction of work emails, Nigel began to relax and open up, sharing how he felt in the changing environment and his thoughts about their future (see Principle 10 – *Reveal More*). With this renewed openness, came a heightened sense of intimacy. I heard many romantic hours were spent star gazing from the hot tub.

My advice for Susan and Nigel and others couples like them— whose time together is regularly compromised by mobile calls, texts or emails—is that on Date Night be generous to each other and leave temptation at home. Yes I do understand that for those of you with young children or unpredictable teens, taking a phone in case of emergencies might be a sensible idea. However, the "I'm bored" calls from a teenager or "just called for a chat" from grown-up children should be fielded. This is not their night.

Date Night versus Responsibilities

A few years ago, Himself was rostered emergency-on-call for forty-eight hour stretches; during these periods, pagers and essential mobiles were ever present and constantly streaming information. Thankfully we had plenty of advance notice of the roster and Date Nights could be planned accordingly. This I suggest doing, to safeguard the romantic intention of Date Night. But, although you can make a supreme effort to schedule a Date Night for when you *don't* have responsibilities (see also Principle 1 – *Get Your Beauty Sleep*), last minute interruptions are possible.

Some of us are better at handling competing demands than others. If a last-minute situation arises, like me, you may find it less stressful and more rewarding to reschedule the Date Night. Yet sometimes situations conspire against you, and it could be simply too late, too costly or too difficult to cancel your Date. I'll give you an example. Cynthia and Clive had booked, months in advance, to join a one-off 'dinner with matching wine' event at Ballymaloe House, Ireland's longest established restaurant. Coveted tickets had sold out within days of release, and for Cynthia this was a much anticipated night (she even enlisted a posse of friends to help select her dress from a list of contending outfits). A few hours before the event, Clive got a request to lead an urgent teleconference, which had to be that very evening! Clive managed the disruption well; indeed so agreeably that Cynthia still felt like his priority and that the romantic intent of the evening wasn't compromised. How on earth did he pull this off, I wondered? By recognising the enormity of the intrusion, involving Cynthia in his thought processes, even giving her some say as to the timing (as he was able to make a call on the start-time of the teleconference). Sensibly, Cynthia suggested as early as possible, so he could then focus on the evening (and her). Naturally she wasn't delighted by the prospect of Clive being absent for much of the dinner, but she recognised that this interruption was not of his making and appreciated his consideration. Before leaving to take the call, Clive made efforts to ensure Cynthia's comfort in his absence, from arranging a glass of bubbly to introducing her to fellow diners, and when he returned from his call, he was fully attentive and admiring of the chosen dress (see Principles 6 and 9). So despite the intrusion, it did end up being a memorable and romantic Date Night. In fact a whole weekend of fun I hear!

We can all take a leaf from Clive's book, and aim to make the best possible moves in the circumstances. If your own Date Night is accosted by late notice of an unavoidable obligation, my advice is to immediately inform your spouse or significant other of the interruption, apologise for it, and calmly discuss with them how to best manage the situation to be as unobtrusive as possible—in other words, don't make a huge fuss! Keep top of mind that, in spite of the interruption, your Date Night and your partner are your priority.

Date Night versus Hobby Night

So far, the interruptions have been people, mobile phones and last minute obligations. Now I turn to the seduction of a highly personal distraction... your hobbies, past-times or passionate interests. If you are a theatre buff, will going to a much-awaited show be more about the *show* than your *Date?* Similarly, if you're fanatical about Tom Jones, will you leave your spouse at the back of the auditorium while you elbow your way forward to toss your underwear on the stage? If you're passionate about dancing, will you discard your mate to the side, in order to 'cut a rug' with that smooth mover? Look, if you both share a passion, such events can be exhilarating and can unite you in your coupledom. (After all, why not His and Hers undies for Tom!) But if the interest is one-sided, take a moment to recognise whether a proposed Date event is really about your partner and romance? If it's more about your hobby, then be respectful and don't earmark it as a Date, for it will surely be a lost cause. Even if you work hard to focus on your partner, it's likely that you will secretly be disheartened at missing a rare opportunity to embrace your passion. And if you embrace your interest, your partner won't feel quite so special. So theatre fans, call it a theatre date, not a Date Night. Avid sporting fans, take your partner by all means but don't set up the expectations of it being a Date. Tom Jones fans, probably best you leave your spouse at home.

Himself's passion is photography. Most people won't leave home without their wallet and keys. My man won't leave home without his camera. I wouldn't ask him to choose between his camera and me—to be honest, I'm not sure I'd like the answer! But we have both learnt that his camera isn't welcomed on Date Night. Here's why… we were visiting the wonderfully romantic old city of Bordeaux, and had put aside an evening for a Date Night. After all we were in France, the country famed for love. We agreed on the restaurant *L'Estacade* for its special location: it sits on stilts above the river and its floor-to-ceiling windows provide spectacular views of the city. What a gorgeous Date Night venue. I timed our dinner reservation so that we could enjoy the sunset. The Date Night started well with a romantic stroll to the restaurant which, we soon discovered, was as remarkable as we hoped. Then as our pre-dinner drink arrived, Himself couldn't help himself— he simply had to accompany his camera to the outside terrace to take photos of the city "while the light is good". At this point I thought, "Fine—it is a lovely setting and it's good that he's enjoying it." Himself returned some fifteen minutes later, by which time I had finished my glass of bubbly (being thirsty after the walk, of course), foregoing our customary Date Night toast (see Principle 8 – *Toast Your Togetherness*). Yet I still believed we were in for a special evening. As hoped for, the magic colours of sunset arrived along with our mains. Rather than sit and marvel at the sky together, Himself abandoned the table, the food and me, to capture the sunset on film. Not knowing how long he was going to be, I sat politely not eating my food, waiting for his return so that we could enjoy our meal together. As I watched my food turn cold,

I felt the romance of the evening also begin to chill. Well not to worry too much, at least there'd be a romantic stroll home, right? I put a brave, but somewhat jaded, face on for the rest of the evening, until it was time for that romantic stroll. We had approached the first bridge, a mere 200 metres from the restaurant, when Himself pulled out his camera to take some 'lights-on-bridge-reflected-in-water' photos. I held my breath, thinking it would be over in a few seconds. But it wasn't. He needed to reset the camera, open the exposure, to get the full effect without using a flash. This technique required even more time—and within me, something finally erupted.

"Are you dating *me*, or your camera?!" I exploded. Not waiting to hear the reply, I stomped alone across the bridge, as fast as my three-inch heels would allow.

It's worth mentioning that this evening didn't immediately translate into 'no cameras on Date Night'. I spent time reflecting on how I could have managed the situation better. Could I have joined him on the terrace and affectionately coaxed him back to the table? Could I have gently given him a clue that the interruption was upsetting me? Should I have lightly negotiated a time limit: two minutes for his photo opportunities? And so on. It was a month after the fateful night in Bordeaux, as we were exiting our apartment for a Date, when I noticed the camera left on the hallway table, I automatically reminded Himself, and he replied that he had chosen not to take it "in case it tempts distraction". We can all create Date Night distractions, yet, like Himself, we can all choose to be self aware and ask ourselves whether our behaviours are contributing to the romantic aim of the evening or not. Good on Him.

In this chapter, I've shared stories about scene stealers: the other people, work interruptions and personal interests that have stolen the romance on Date Night. I hope these stories will help you avoid distractions and prioritise your partner so that there is a real chance of romance occurring. Whilst I've covered some obvious and not so obvious issues, think carefully about what adversely affects *your* romance. Do you invite distraction by engaging with your phone, engaging with strangers or even engaging with your personal hobbies? Well, remember who you prized enough to marry (or the equivalent) and that this is your Date Night with that person.

Actions:

- Identify what things are likely to steal the romance on your intimate evening.
- Protect your Date Night from these distractions. Start by reserving your phone for critical calls only.
- Prioritise your beloved when you must share the evening with others – for example, use praise or a caring (but appropriate!) touch.
- Maintain a focus on your partner during those unavoidable phone calls; keep eye contact and smile.
- Compensate for interruptions—be apologetic, then fully attentive.
- Watch out for Date events that are more about a personal interest or hobby than about your partner.

We are all vulnerable in various degrees to distraction. You can do your best to manage and avoid the temptation, yet over the course of many Date Nights, intrusions *will* happen. It'll come down to your ability to handle the distraction and maintaining focus on your partner, in order to preserve the romantic intent of the evening. By taking this Date Night Vitamin you will *Keep Your Eyes Focused on the Prize (Your Beloved)*. And don't forget what a good prize that is!

15. Take a Break from 'Decisions We Must Make'

"It's much easier for me to make major life, multi-million dollar decisions, than it is to decide on a carpet for my front porch."
— Oprah Winfrey

Lesson from your early dates: No shared life (yet) meant no decision-making debates.

Relationship bliss involves decision-making. Decision-making on Date Night does not usually make for romantic bliss. In fact it can rapidly downgrade your Date to 'just another evening debating XYZ'. At best, you might reach a decision. At worst, dealing with major dilemmas might direct you into an emotional minefield. Such conversations are risky to an evening's goal of intimacy; they take the focus off enjoying each other and can even cause rifts between you.

Take your mind back to when you were on the singles scene and going out on those very first dates—how much joint decision-making do you remember? That's right—where to meet, what to do, whether to share a dessert or a cab is about as intense as it got. Perhaps even whether to 'have breakfast together', if you get my drift. Essentially, back when there was no shared life, there was little requirement for making major decisions together. You were insulated from such a distraction and could concentrate on the matter at hand, which was focusing on your date and exploring the opportunity for romance.

Now fast forward to today: you're in an established relationship and sharing a life together, and there's a continuous stream of questions that need to be answered.

The big fundamental decisions: Shall we try for a third baby? Shall we move house? Or country? When and where shall we retire? The more practical decisions: Where shall we go on holiday? Do we really need a new car? Wooden flooring, lino or carpet? Shall we let little Johnny quit piano lessons?

A Good Decision versus a Good Date

Many questions need consideration and an agreement to be reached. Depending on the importance of the issue at hand, whether you are thinking the same way or are opposed, even your individual personalities, all have a bearing on how that decision-making pans out. Indeed, these things can also affect whether the discussion is likely to be resolved easily, turn into a raging debate, become a bone of contention, or wind up with someone sleeping on the couch.

Remember in Principle 1– *Get Your Beauty Sleep*, I talk about the all-importance of energy for being able to perform your best on your Date. Studies into decision-making processes show that the best decisions require focus and energy too. When you're tired, and/or haven't acquainted yourself with the details, you are more likely to make a conservative, or a 'no to low change' decision.[25] Following logic, if making decisions on Date Night, either you will expend vital energy on this decision-making at the expense of the Date, or your focus on the Date will compromise the quality of your decision outcome. Either way, don't mix the two.

It's worth side-stepping here for a moment to make this point: involving the other in your personal decision-making—like solving a work dilemma, hobby quandary or other issue that is independent of your partner—is a sign of your friendship; it shows trust and respect. Ultimately though, on a Date you want to move to that level *beyond* the friendship, to the more intimate and exclusive conversations in which you might reveal more about yourself. Or if you're on the listening end, to gently probe for deeper insights and encourage him or her with compliments and praise (see Principle 9 – *The Etiquette of Flattery* and Principle 10 – *Reveal More*). This can lead to a meaningful connection, a heightened sense of attachment. So if solving dilemmas together is an aspect of your *friendship*, Date Night is where you up your game for your *romance*.

Focused on romance, there are some joint decisions that have an intimate twist, and can consolidate your connection on Date Night. "Shall we sign-up for salsa classes?" (assuming you both love to dance) or "Where might we go for our anniversary holiday?" or merely "More champagne, dear?" But these are not the subject of *Take a Break from 'Decisions We Must Make'*.

Some say that agreeing on the big stuff can bring you closer and help you feel more aligned and connected. *I* say that is true if *and only if*, the essential 'agreement' factor is present. When you broach any decision you can't always be assured of like-mindedness.

What this boils down to is this: if you decide to raise a major dilemma on your Date Night, you'll need to be fairly convinced the response will align with yours. Alternatively, you need to be ready to accommodate your partner's potentially different perspective. Let's say, for example, you want to launch a discussion on whether you and your spouse should move back into your childhood home after the passing of your parents. Now that's a major joint decision. This prospect could be contentious, raising differing opinions and potential conflict; which, if you remember from Principle 13 – *Be a Lover Not a Fighter,* should best be avoided on Date Night. Yet in a different scenario, your partner has regularly expressed great awe of your family home. In this case you're more confident of an aligned response, and you can feel better about bringing this up.

So ease of agreement is what you're looking for, if raising a life-altering theme on Date Night. The big emotion-filled decisions can be a dicey Date strategy. Progress only if you are fairly sure of your alignment on the issue, or if you yourself don't mind agreeing.

If you find that you are the receiver of a meaty question, and you sense your perspectives might not match up, the safest thing to do is to shelve it for another day—and preferably not a Date Night. By saying "It's a big issue, and I would like to give it my full consideration", you should buy time and a safe departure from potential conflict on Date Night.

Jonathan, aged fifty-one, and Emily, thirty-four, were married just three years when Emily raised the subject of starting a family. Emily is Jonathan's second wife, and at this time his children from his first marriage were just finishing high school. Before he embarked on his current marriage with Emily, Jonathan had expressed that he didn't want the burden of young children during his retirement—so when Emily revealed her desire to start a family, this was an annoyance to him. Yet Emily had convinced herself that Jonathan would welcome the prospect; she had observed how attentive he was with his girls and how he relished his parenting role. In the end, they did agree to have two children (Jonathan looks and feels younger as a result), but it took many months of discussion and heated debate before they finally reached alignment. For Emily to broker this discussion on a Date Night would certainly have caused a departure from the romantic objective of the evening. This is bound to be a topic that rises amongst many couples, but as this Principle recommends, it's not ideal Date Night fodder (unless, as I've mentioned, you are ultra sure of the agreement factor).

When it comes to the less fundamental, and the smaller or more practical decisions, you might think that there is less emotional investment in the outcome, and that you're less likely to stray into conflict zones. However, be warned: sometimes we are more invested in the small stuff than we are in the big decisions. Like Oprah, as quoted at the start of the chapter (it's harder for her to decide on a carpet than major deals), I will fiercely fight for refurbishing the dining-room chairs, but I really don't mind which country we live in (as long as my chairs come too).

Personality Differences and Decision-Making

Shall we do something new? Or stick to the same? Decision-making often involves confronting change. Some people's personalities mean that they actively seek change, whereas other personalities don't. And a suggested change that is not of our own volition can raise resistance and bring out strong reactions. Proposing moving that photo of Great-Aunt Meryl or switching the SUV to a two-seater might be met with a resounding "No". Turning your son's bedroom into a craft room might also elicit a "No" (even though he now has his own house!). Sometimes change like that is actually for the best. So you'll need to set aside a time and occasion in order to win-over your dissenting spouse. But Date Night is not it. See later in this chapter for more on timing.

So maybe you haven't received that "No". Yet have you found your attempts at joint decision-making result in any of the following:

withdrawal, irritation, a rigorous examination of the minutiae, too-rapid agreement without real consideration, or getting stuck in contemplation? Spare yourself on Date Night, as these point to different personalities' decision-making reactions.[26] As a couple it is unlikely that you both share the exact same personality preferences so your approach to decision-making will vary. If you are assured that you *and* your partner will both get a buzz by reaching a decision, then good for you. (Watch carefully, it can be all too easy for the excited person to assume the other is too.) From this platform of enthusiasm, accomplishment and alignment then you may find that romance comes readily—that is if you don't get side-tracked sorting out the decision's logistics.

When Himself and I were renovating our house, there were numerous decisions that needed to be made. Himself, thankfully, tended to the project management type decisions without my involvement. Where he needed my input on finishes and kitchen layout (I love to entertain whilst cooking), he would be clearly frustrated by my time-intensive need to carefully research and evaluate all options. I have heard Himself complain that he could have rebuilt our house ten times in the space it took me to reach a single decision. During this time, our (pre-Manifesto) Date Nights were compromised with horridly unromantic discussions along the lines of whether the kitchen bench should be one and a half or two inches thick. Good grief. Not only did the dull content of this discussion extinguish any flame of romance, our contrary decision-making styles added frustration and irritation to our Dates. For some personalities like my own, with the need to explore all the alternatives, decision-making can be exhausting task. For other personalities, it's a satisfying activity—the closing of an outstanding issue can settle the mind and leave them with a sense of peace. Put the two types into one relationship, and someone's going to get grumpy.

To illustrate further: according to Myers Briggs (the world's most applied personality tool) all people can be divided into two lifestyle preferences, called Judging and Perceiving, which have distinctly different approaches to decision-making. A person with Judging preferences tends to like quick closure. They will find satisfaction in the resolution of an issue and might be quoted as saying "a good decision is a fast decision". Whereas someone with a Perceiving preference might believe in "no decision before the right time".

Cynthia (a Perceiving type) is less inclined to hold back decisive Clive (a Judging type) on Date Night. Observing Principle 12 – *Negativity No-Nos*, Cynthia rightly focuses on the positive to preserve and build on the warm vibes of the night. This is great for the Date but doesn't always make for good decisions. Blushingly, Cynthia divulged to me the details about a fabulous but flawed Date Night. They were totally loved-up, and through the spectrum of romance-fuelled rose-tinted glasses (*and* a bottle of rose wine) Clive suggested that they buy a significant piece of art from the walls of the restaurant. Not wanting to spoil his evening, she agreed. The next morning, they returned to collect their purchase, and were dismayed to find—with the clarity of daylight—that their 'art' was a poor poster-type reproduction. Clive was too embarrassed to even take it home! Still, it was a good Date—just a whole lot more expensive than usual.

Taking Time for 'Decisions We Must Make'

So you're the type who prefers closure? The temptation to call up a *Decision We Must Make* on Date Night is the strongest for you. Here you are, face to face with your beloved and household mate, who is giving you their undivided attention. What better time could there be? Answer: just about any *other* time. Hold your tongue, and learn to quell that desire. This is easier if you can identify alternative times or opportunities to discuss the pros and cons of your issue and reach a solution. My friend Alison, married to management executive Tim, has a Judging personality and likes to reach closure on decisions. She was fully aware that in her previous quest for conclusions, she couldn't hold back from raising questions when she had Tim as a captive audience. Date Nights were far too tempting. Alison now manages this tendency by closing outstanding decisions at the weekend prior to a Date, and she is purposeful about where and when she engages Tim in those discussions. For those decisions that require thought, she'll give him advance notice of the subject. Then they'll set aside an hour or two on Sunday afternoon to tackle the topic. What might work for you?

Actions:

- Decide to only raise major decisions if you are confident of an aligned perspective.
- Deflect emotionally-charged dilemmas and postpone these for another time.
- Address pressing decisions prior to Date Night.
- Recognise that you might have different approaches to decision-making, and that your quest for closure might exhaust your partner. Either way, steer away from decisions on Date Night.

For those of you with hectic schedules and rare opportunities for time together, you can surely see how Date Night can be a highly seductive setting for your decision-making. So do be mindful of the risks: you may be inviting poor decisions, conflict due to differences in opinions, and frustration due to contrary approaches—all which make a dent in romantic intent. On your next Date, *Take a Break from 'Decisions We Must Make'* and *do* avoid practical decisions, as they can transform a Date into merely a domestic evening. I'll talk about the danger of 'domestics' in the next chapter.

16. Shelve Those Domestic Details

"Romance is the glamour which turns the dust of everyday life into a golden haze."
— Carolyn Gold Heilbrun

Lesson from your early dates: You certainly wouldn't bore your date with your domestic/admin details!

The mistress runs a seductive hand down your husband's arm, nibbles on his ear, and in a voice husky with wine and romantic anticipation, whispers, "Darling… don't you think the insurance premiums are too high? I'm sure you can find a better deal elsewhere."

This is fiction of course. In place of the mistress (gender not withstanding), there is you. Not the 'other woman' or 'other man', but the 'other half'. OK, the insurance needs updating. But does it need to be discussed on Date Night? On an evening designated for romance, such a dreary domestic detail is a fish out of water. Regardless of who is romancing whom, a conversation about insurance clearly has no place on Date Night.

Don't underestimate the potency of this Date Night Vitamin. Raising routine admin and household stuff *diminishes your alluring self* and *suffocates romance*. This is the common curse of the established couple. You may as well date with your apron on. When you *Shelve Those Domestic Details*, you save your Date from a platonic fate.

We can learn from the Renaissance-era masters of romance: the courtesans and the male equivalent, chevalier servants.[27] They were independent, well-educated and respected for their charm and ability to entertain (as well as their artistic sexual practices). Until the eighteenth century, courtesans and chevalier servants had the responsibility of paying amorous attention to royalty and the upper classes. They were essentially professionals at the art of romance. So when you are anticipating or reviewing Date Night, reflect on your approach to the evening. Are you more of a 'romantic maestro' or a 'dutiful but distant' or just plain 'domestic' spouse? The bottom line is... household administration has *got* to be the antithesis to romance.

Just take a look at the *Oxford Dictionary* definition of the R word: *'a quality or feeling of mystery, excitement, and remoteness from everyday life'*. From that alone, you can surely recognise the problem with discussing domestic issues on Date Night. Wouldn't you agree that routine tasks, to-do-lists and calendar co-ordination are unlikely to fan any fires of romance? Then why is it that so many couples are frequently lured into these passion-killing conversations?

Domestic and Proud

I've heard people say that this is how they define themselves as an established couple; through their domestic arrangements and discourse. It's the difference between being lovers and being partners. For some it's a badge of honour, marking the fulfilment of their aspirations for a committed relationship. I spoke to Jean-Claude who was in a long term relationship with Jeremy for ten years before they parted ways. Jean-Claude says that he was possibly in love with being in a domestic relationship, where he took much pride in the care-taking role. He would happily focus conversation on household issues to boost his sense of achievement as a homemaker.

The person who assumes responsibility for the domestic details might be a full-time house-wife or house-husband, an enthusiastic homemaker, or indeed a martyr to the cause. They could well find reporting on the household situation to be a way of affirming their contribution and role in the partnership. But just as you wouldn't hijack a Date Night talking about work or your hobbies, (see Principle 14 – *Keep Your Eyes on the Prize (Your Beloved)*) then you shouldn't rattle on about domestic chores—or even domestic passions.

In the same category as household admin, I place 'diary checking', which some might call 'schedule aligning' or 'calendar co-ordination'. Sure, it's essential to the smooth running of any domestic operation—you need to agree on dates to visit your in-laws, when to schedule the window cleaner or identify which days you're both free. Yet it hardly belongs in an evening's romantic itinerary. For some of you, getting task closure or synchronising calendars may be an easier source of satisfaction than investing energy on the less tangible pursuit of intimacy.

Twenty years married, Diana, a publisher, and Paul, a reporter, are often vulnerable to diary discussions. Diana's frantic schedule involves numerous charity engagements, work commitments and extensive friends and family obligations. A single free day in a fortnight is a rarity for this fast-paced woman. So if she has an evening alone with Paul, Diana will enthusiastically engage him in diary planning. For her this activity is hugely satisfying, as she gets important closure on their joint availability so she can then arrange more of her events or alternative activities.

However, it is not necessarily so satisfying for Paul. I suspect he finds it a chore and given a choice, he'd prefer they just focus on enjoying dinner together: the food, wine, music, and each other. And failing that, he would rather be watching television. Such admin discussions, like diary checking and household issues might be satisfying to one partner, maybe even both—but it comes at the cost of real intimacy.

Alternative Times for Routine Admin

Obviously there's necessity and practicality in doing so, but surely there's a more suitable time and setting for domestic administration, such as over breakfast at the kitchen table, before dinner in your home office, or on any regular old *non*-Date Night evening. Himself and I put to rest our admin on Saturday mornings. You'll see us at our local deli and once replete with espresso (and croissants) we'll extract our diaries, 'to do' lists and agree on our forthcoming commitments. Neither of us are particularly keen on these discussions, nor the resultant tasks, so staging it in our favourite deli helps to smooth the process. Let's say you're on a Date Night, and your partner raises some admin, or worse still, produces their diary or smartphone calendar. If it can be covered in a minute or two then fine, but otherwise gently remind them that it's Date Night and suggest an alternate time. Diana solved her dilemma by covering pressing items when she and Paul are commuting downtown together, and then clearing diary issues as a pre-dinner activity. Similarly, Alison talks over these items with Tim as they walk home from the train station. Another couple, Laura and Jeff with four children, have found that a mid-week email exchange is efficient; saving their precious together time from being compromised by copious admin.

So, assuming that alternative times and places are available for this kind of conversation, why do many couples *still* surrender to household details on a special night for two? There are a couple of likely reasons.

One—it's a low-effort, safe discourse. Two—it can act as a shield to intimacy and saves you from going outside your comfort zone and trying something new.

Established Patterns of Conversation

Your household or domestic conversations have been established since the beginning of your live-in relationship, so they are safe, easy, and a familiar way of communicating. Practical and administrative motives provide little opportunity to get passionate. When did you last rip each other's clothes off over the making of a grocery list? (Although shopping for cars or new clothes might be very exciting for some.) No, this dialogue is a far more reserved and comfortable forum. In short, it is the lazy option. Do you find it easier to retreat to this low-effort, practised patter than focus on your Date Night Decorum (Part 2: Principles 6-11), such as *Reveal More?* The lights are low, evocative music enhances the mood, yet you feel more comfortable chatting about the household budget, or the impending visit from the in-laws. Lo and behold, you've put romance on the back-burner once again.

This is an example of domestic chatter acting as a shield to intimacy. Being affectionate and sharing meaningful sentiments can be challenging for some people, for numerous reasons. Maybe they feel awkward because they're not practised in expressing this side of themselves, or they're not confident of the response. On a less positive note, they might not be motivated to deepen the relationship because they're no longer interested in romance. (See *Dealing with 'Date Night Resistance'*, specifically from page 209 where I talk about those who are not romantically inclined; those who may enjoy being together for their wider family life or simply the friendship they share and value.)

Ralph and Helen, an accountant and a community advisor married twenty-nine years, are committed Christians who take their marital vows and parental duties seriously. Ralph travels from their home in Leeds to London for work; he stays during the week, travelling two-and-a-half hours home on Friday. As it happens, Helen's part-time job at the community centre means that she works most Saturdays. This means their time together is limited to Sundays, which is absorbed by church and the wider family. Helen tells me that their 'talk time' is very much focused on admin, tasks and scheduling. One week might result in the purchase of a new Hoover, the next week they'd plan to select and install new shower doors. I sense that Helen and Ralph are awkward with their amorous selves and find it easier to embrace shared domestic duties than romantic endeavours. For relationships like theirs, with entrenched patterns of domestic dialogue, if they want to explore a greater level of intimacy, they will need to set aside *separate* time for household details, and define some time and space for romance. Here, the Date Night Manifesto is your friend! It can provide a reassuring guide for navigating intimate conversations, focusing attention on just each other, and while that might be a little awkward initially, with time you will find yourself growing more relaxed and able to express your affection.

We can summarise, then, that discussing domestic details is seductive for admin aficionados and those less at ease with their romantic selves—it provides safe, easy and comfortable conversation. And that for those in longer relationships, you're likely to have established set patterns of communicating on shared household issues. From energy-saving and internet provision through to dental fees and refuse collections, you can contentedly pass an evening with hardly any effort—and, I'd suggest, hardly any romance.

This then is your challenge: rather than merely maintaining your comfortable domestic self, draw upon your alluring self. Yes, you *do* have one of those in you. (It will be discovered when you discard the figurative apron and leave your diary in a drawer.)

As mentioned in the introduction, we live in a society where there is an expectation of romance within a marriage. Rather than settle for a loveless marriage or partnership to serve a societal, religious or even familial purpose, at the heart of it you need to satisfy your own desires, and you are less likely to compromise on achieving these.

"But," you worry, "without our usual domestic dialogue, what are we going to talk about? There'll be... silence!" Fear not. *Shelving Those Domestic Details* creates space for your charming self. Expressing your more seductive side is made easy thanks to the Manifesto's Date Night Decorum (Part 2: Principles 6-12). These Principles coach you to be attentive and appreciative, to give thanks and compliments, to show your value of the relationship, and to reveal more about yourself. Also *let* there be silence... you might be pleased by what might comes up,[28] when you're open to it. The Beach Boys sang about silence being golden. A lot of people are afraid of this, and fill silences with inane chatter which often sounds like domestic patter. See silences as a golden opportunity for you to check that your body language is warm and approachable: caring smiles, close proximity, and so on. Himself often removes his tie and releases the button on his collar, signifying his comfort with me and his surroundings. (I find this quite sexy!)

I mentioned in the previous chapter about those who find Date Night too tempting a chance to get closure on decisions. That goes for outstanding domestic items too. Many busy people develop checklists of tasks in order to keep on top of their domestic life. Reminders to send birthday cards, buy more laundry liquid, pick up paint swatches for the kitchen cupboards, call the mortgage broker about refinancing, organise a babysitter for next week's Date Night. Oh and when you're feeling a little too time-poor, an opportunity to tick off items together might be *irresistible*. However, on Date Night, leave the list alone, even if it is in need of attention. As advised in Principle 15 —*Take a Break from 'Decisions We Must Make'* regarding the bigger issues, try and make time in advance of your Date to resolve any pressing domestic issues.

You simply *must* recognise your to-do list as a diversion and distraction from your intimate endeavours. Remind yourself that a masterful seducer would hardly launch into an inventory of domestic chores. Cleopatra may well have seduced two great Roman leaders, but I doubt she would've prattled on about the nitty-gritty of running a kingdom.

Getting Away with the Teensiest Bit of Admin

What's this? I don't practise what I preach? Well I do have to confess that Himself and I seldom get a perfect score for this Principle. We have found it difficult *not* to cover a little essential household activity during the course of a Date Night, and you might find it tricky too. I've popped out a "Before I forget, please remind me to collect the dry cleaning tomorrow", or "Can you pick up Jim from the airport at 5pm?" But to be fair, it's normally an urgent reminder. If I don't collect the dry cleaning tomorrow, I'll have no decent suits for that corporate event the following day. If Himself can't collect Jim, I need to quickly make other plans.

I find that any administration is mentioned *in passing* when we are diverted from more intimate conversation, such as when transitioning from the taxi to the venue, waiting to be seated or collecting our coats. If a reminder simply must be passed on, try to restrict yourself to an in-between moment; paying car parking fees, getting into an elevator, waiting to cross the road, and so on. Soon it will become easier to combat the temptations this Principle covers.

Remember that Date Night requires energy – so when you are tempted to discuss admin at length, *recognise* that you are taking the lazy option. Routine admin and check lists are fine for any ordinary evening, but be mindful that this is Date Night. The focus is on each other, not a cross-examination of the credit card bill. The shared intent is intimacy, not reorganising timetables so someone can be home for the plumber.

Actions:

- Keep the romantic maestros in mind when approaching Date Night.
- Recognise domestic tasks as a diversion from romantic endeavours.
- Suggest shelving it for later—an alternative time for its discussion—if your partner raises an admin topic (unless it can be covered in two minutes).
- Resolve domestic issues in advance of the Date, especially if you're an admin aficionado or list lover.
- Mention admin only if it's urgent, for instance an important reminder for the next day. And keep it to a fleeting moment.

Save your Date from the dreaded curse of the established couple – domestic dialogue. Once you have *Shelved Those Domestic Details* you'll find it easier to bring on the charm, the appreciation and really work on the romantic attachment. Challenge yourself, conjure in your mind a seventeenth century courtesan or chevalier servant in your mind, put yourself in their elegant satin shoes, and try being more dedicated to the art of romance.

DATE NIGHT ACCESSORIES

Date Idea-Sparkers

Dates are all about you feeling special and making your partner feel loved and treasured. With this in mind, some dating activities can be more successful than others!

As a rule of thumb, when sparking ideas for your next Date, think of Date occasions that in themselves are special and memorable. But *also* think how you can maximise the opportunity to demonstrate your Date Night Decorum (Principles from Part Two). Specifically:

Principle 6 – *Hang off Their Every Word*
Principle 7 – *Every Venue Has a Silver Lining*
Principle 8 – *Toast Your Togetherness*
Principle 9 – *The Etiquette of Flattery*
Principle 10 – *Reveal More (but No Strip Tease—Yet)*
Principle 11 – *Wanted: Good Sense of Humour*

Excelling at any or all of these requires sufficient 'talk time'. With this in mind, Date Night ideas such as dinner or drinks will fare better than the movies or live-music Date.

The table below shows you those dating ideas which readily activate the Date Night Manifesto's Principles. Date ideas marked with a ✓ will make your Date Night success easier. Where there is an X below a Principle, you will need to pay more attention and invest more effort in this Principle to achieve a romantic outcome. Where there is no ✓ or X, it means that particular Principle is not necessarily affected by that specific Date idea.

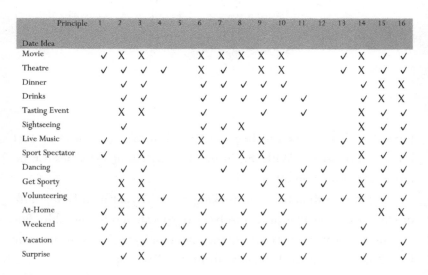

Date Idea	1	2	3	4	5	6	7	8	9	10	11	12	13	14	15	16
Movie	✓	X	X			X	X	X	X	X			✓	X	✓	✓
Theatre	✓	✓	✓	✓		X	✓		X	X			✓	X	✓	✓
Dinner		✓	✓			✓	✓	✓	✓	✓				✓	X	X
Drinks		✓	✓			✓	✓	✓	✓	✓	✓			✓	X	X
Tasting Event		X	X			✓			✓		✓			X	✓	✓
Sightseeing		✓				✓	✓	X						X	✓	✓
Live Music	✓	✓	✓			X	✓		X				✓	X	✓	✓
Sport Spectator	✓		X			X		X	X					X	✓	✓
Dancing		✓	✓			✓	✓	✓		✓	✓	✓	✓	✓	✓	✓
Get Sporty		X	X					✓	X	✓	✓			X	✓	✓
Volunteering		X	X	✓		X	X	X		X		✓	✓	X	✓	✓
At-Home	✓	X	X			✓		✓	✓	✓					X	X
Weekend	✓	✓	✓	✓	✓	✓	✓	✓	✓	✓	✓			✓		✓
Vacation	✓	✓	✓	✓	✓	✓	✓	✓	✓	✓	✓			✓		✓
Surprise		✓	X			✓		✓	✓		✓			✓		✓

Now that you have seen the overview, here's my no-holds-barred analysis of the more popular Dates. You'll find that caveats and conditions are outlined, helping you to make an informed decision about which Date Night ideas really complement you.

Movie Date — *multi-screen complexes, retro-picture houses, film festival, outdoor screenings*

Pros:

- Can help you re-energise for later in the Date (you can even catch forty winks).
- Provides a bonding opportunity if movie-going is an avid joint hobby.
- Fosters interesting conversations or a deeper level of dialogue, if the content of the movie is romantic or meaningful. For example after watching *The Bucket List*, a comedy-drama about two terminally ill men, Himself and I began exploring our own hopes and dreams for the future.
- Will be reasonably inexpensive—unless you splash out on VIP suites, Gold Class seats or silver-plated popcorn.

Cons:

- Limits talking time. If the Date Night is solely the movie, it can prove a distraction to the Principles of the Manifesto. Time spent watching the big screen is time when you're not being fully focused on your partner, making him or her laugh or exchanging affection-inducing endearments.
- Could turn out to be horribly unromantic. The movie content, that is. Stay clear of movies that will leave you traumatised, irritated or irate. Also try to avoid those mind-messing, seemingly-devoted-spouse-has-secret-life storylines.
- Might not be seen as special or romantic. Your local multiplex cinema, built without any architectural contribution, can be a highly commercial and soul-destroying experience. Try seeking something out of the ordinary, for example: attending the opening night of a

movie, going to a film festival, or seeing a movie in a unique cinema (I love the independent retro picture houses).

- Can represent a lazy option as it doesn't require much thought. We all feel special when someone makes an effort.

Theatre Date – *play, broadway show, comedy, opera, ballet, musical*

Pros:

- Can be seen as a quite a treat!
- Signifies an evident opportunity to get dressed up.
- Gives you the chance to chat during the intermission—that is, if you're not stuck in a long queue for the loo!
- Can be romantic in its content. From Tchaikovsky's ballet *The Nutcracker* to the musical *Beauty and the Beast* or the ever-popular *The Sound of Music*, there are plenty of shows that will make your heart swell.

Cons:

- May be expensive. So look out for half-price deals, or midweek specials.
- Offers little talking time, much like the movie Date (see page 181); and this means you can fail to reconnect and fan the flame of romance. You could opt for a pre-show dinner, but in my experience these are often rushed affairs where the emphasis is on getting through the meal and bill payment in time and *not* on each other. Just be wild and have a very late supper! Or skip the meal and arrange a relaxing post-theatre drink instead.
- May get uncomfortable. Watch out for those four-hour operas. And pay attention to nineteenth century theatres; they may look charming, but were designed pre-air conditioning and for a small-framed, short-legged audience.

- Could turn out to be a bit bleak. I went to see the play *Children of the Poor* and sadly the poor just got poorer. Such performances might erode your appetite for romance.
- Can be unbalanced—one of you may be more enthusiastic than the other. Who is being dragged along?

Dining Date — *dinner, breakfast, brunch, lunch, picnic*

Pros:

- Maximises the talking time on a Date, which actively supports the Manifesto's intimacy-building Intentions.
- Can be seen as special and romantic. Remember to choose someplace that isn't your everyday dining spot.
- Allows you to dress to impress.
- Eating is enjoyable... and practical. We all need to eat! And it doesn't necessarily need to be dinner; any meal could become a Date.
- Lets you attach another Date activity. To really set the Date apart, add in a visit to a gallery or see a show. You could even catch a sports event.

Cons:

- Creates the risk, if attending a buffet, of eating 'past your fill', which could lead to drowsiness and a bedroom retreat minus the bedroom action. Not all dining options are designed for romance.
- Can be expensive. But it doesn't need to be. With some research you will always find something romantic to match the capacity of your wallet. In my experience some of the pricier options can be too clinical or corporate for a romantic dinner for two.

Restaurant reviewers tend to agree; I recall a Dublin publication that highlighted mostly budget options in its recommendations for that city's romantic dining.

- Could be less comfortable for some people, especially a lengthy dinner. In this case, mix up the Date venues to make it more interesting. Enjoy pre-dinner drinks at an alternative bar before you proceed to the restaurant, or skip dessert and take a post-dinner beverage elsewhere.

Drinks Date — *cocktail bar, wine bar, cosy pub, old haunt from yesteryear*

Pros:

- Energises your Date—a buzzy bar vibe can lift the spirits.
- Revitalises you after a hectic day—alcohol (in moderation of course) can restore a good mood.
- Can be bonding if it's a night spot where you have romantic memories—with each other, that is.
- Creates plenty of opportunity for talk time—assuming the background music isn't too loud! As mentioned under the dinner Date, talk time crucially supports the Manifesto's intimacy-building Intentions.
- Might kindle romance. Many bars seem to have a knack for this; think glamorous hotel lobby bars, discreet cocktail bars, and those old-fashioned pubs with private nooks.
- Connecting drinks with other activities is a great way to start or end your Date (or grab a breather in the middle).

Cons:

- Could lay your Date open to distractions. Watch out for this! The

Sports TV at a bar may prove irresistible for sport fans. Your neighbourhood hang out, or workplace happy hour, might turn your evening for two into a party of four or more.

- Can turn sour if alcohol intolerance arises. For some people there's a fine-line between being in good spirits and legless. The latter will compromise your Date.
- May be uncomfortable, especially if you're standing in heels, or jostling to get served. So get to the bar early, reserve the best seats, or just choose a lesser known night spot.
- Could be costly, especially cocktails, top shelf spirits and fine wines. If budget is a consideration, there are always inexpensive drinking outlets. But be careful not to downgrade the allure of the setting so that it's no longer special. I challenge you to *not* elect a cheaper venue so you can drink more, but instead choose to drink less in a nicer venue.

Tasting Events – *sampling teas and coffees, cheeses, baked goods, wines, whiskys*

Pros:

- Engenders good spirits (quite literally, if you're doing a whisky tasting).
- Raises a sensual appreciation. You will be aware of all your taste sensations of course, but the aim for a tasting Date is to pay attention to your other half's preferences.
- Lets you play and experiment.
- Can be inexpensive (depending on the tasting event).

Cons:

- Can be more focused on the tasting subject than learning about each other. So keep your beloved centre stage and carve out time for that all-important intimacy-building talk.

- Could involve being sociable with a wider group; though this can be nice, it poses a diversion to your romantic objective.
- May not be a particularly romantic venue. Avoid tasting experiences held at drab conference centres or anonymous exhibition halls; rather, elect a venue which offers a hint of romantic charm, such as wine-tasting in a vineyard or old cellar. Himself and I were delighted to discover a Scottish whisky tasting being held fireside in the lounge of a historic hotel, complete with kilt-wearing whisky expert.

Sightseeing Date – *place of interest, art gallery, museum, historic site, botanic gardens*

Pros:

- Can often be free, or inexpensive.
- Tailoring the duration of the visit can provide a more enjoyable experience. Agree on a time-limit if you don't want the whole day to be taken up with visiting a major site or exhibition.
- Lets you incorporate dinner or drinks. Museums, galleries and botanic gardens often have quaint cafes, tea-rooms and occasionally even a swish bar!
- Expressing your reactions to the art or exhibits can provide an opportunity to learn more about the other. Himself and I have an annual Date at Tate Britain Museum's Turner Prize Exhibition. The finalists' sensational art always provokes emotional responses and provides fodder for animated conversation.
- Can be memorable and demonstrate thought. Especially when you find something to excite you both. There is an attraction for

everyone, whether it's wildlife and science-based exhibitions, a historical house or other local curiosities.

Cons:

- May be more focused on the sightseeing experience than reconnecting with each other. So remember to add in dinner or drinks, and find time to appreciate your mate.
- Can cause boredom to one of you, if the other has a tendency to dwell intensely on each exhibit. In this case I would avoid visiting a large exhibition. Choose a small exhibition; I went to an opening recently that only had three pieces (Himself was visibly relieved!).
- Could be discomfort-inducing. It's not always pleasurable to stride a vast acreage of museum space, especially in stilettos—which are not exactly desirable for studying azaleas at the botanic gardens either. So dress appropriately and keep your Date smile intact.

Live Music Date — *big gig, classical concert, jazz club, acoustic set, choral group*

Pros:

- May well be a fabulous Date if it's a group or musician that you both have a fond association with. Remember Tim and Alison, who have 'White Dress' by The Fairport Convention as 'their' song? Attending a Fairport Convention show would be a great Date for this couple.
- Is normally seen as a special occasion.
- Can be romantic depending on the music and the atmosphere. Himself and I use to frequent a basement jazz club in London; the intimate setting and the double bass player epitomised my idea of early twentieth century romance.

- Gives you the chance to be thoughtful about your attire — whether going to the big gig or the classical concert.

Cons:

- Puts your focus ultimately on the music and not on each other. So make use of the waiting time, intermission or breaks between sets to be attentive to your mate.
- Could create a mild 'disharmony' if one person is notably more interested in the musician than the other. If so, use the concert as an opportunity to learn more about their musical connection. Or pick performers that you both love.
- Can pose a problem for those not keen on being on their feet for too long. Some venues are standing only, so watch the comfort factor. For those bigger events, consider the queue for drinks, the condition of the loos, and the general push and shove of the crowd.
- Could create grumpiness during the often protracted waiting time for performances to start! This can be fine if you're prepared, but if you're in an outdoor arena and getting chilled as the night sets in, you could have your nose out of joint before the show even begins. So wise up, come equipped and in the right state of mind for enjoyment, in spite of the more tedious aspects. If that sounds tricky then do as I do and avoid large concerts for Date Night.
- Limits your talking time. Chatting during the concert or show is likely to upset fervent music lovers. Where possible, organise drinks or dinner around the music event to secure a richer discussion.
- Might be associated with transport hassles, especially the big gigs, and this itself could mute any blush of desire.

Sport Spectator Date — *live events, big screen showings, television viewing*

Pros:

• Can be energising and fun.
• Creates a great way of connecting. Himself and I both like a flutter at the horse races. Ladies Day, for which spectators dress up to the nines, donning colourful hats and sprightly fascinators, makes a sport occasion into a fine Date occasion.
• If it's one person's passion, it could be a way for your partner to reveal more about him or herself.
• Cultivates inspiration by watching athletes perform at the highest level. It can prompt interesting discussions about what you admire in past and current sport stars.
• Going to a famous sports venue can be a unique and memorable experience.

Cons:

• Being emotionally invested in the result of the sporting event could mean the Date's success is linked to the sports score.
• Focusing more on the game can mean less focus on you as a couple.
• Watching the sport on television might not be special unless you plan some romantic accoutrements. Viewing Wimbledon's televised tennis final at home could be romanced-up with the help of strawberries and cream, pink fizz or iced tea—and if you're game, a tennis dress!
• Could be tiresome for a partner who is not so interested in the sport. Yet many sporting events do hold appeal for the less enthusiastic spectator. The Superbowl, for example, is more like a festival than a sports competition. The Rowing Regatta at Henley is a divine setting to picnic and drink Pimms. And on a different

note, but ever so romantic, Himself and I have risen before dawn and driven into the desert near Abu Dhabi to watch the Camel Races; whilst these prancing foaming gangly beasts are bewitching, the light and mood at sunrise is just as captivating.

Dancing Date — *nightclubs, live-music events, parties, dinner dances, formal functions, community socials*

Pros:

- Connects you intimately! Whether it's a saucy salsa, cheek-to-cheek tango, spry waltz or just a slow smooch around the floor, dancing as a couple can be the height of romance.
- Involves just the two of you.
- Releases feel good endorphins, which fully support the romantic aims of the evening. With close physical connection and racing endorphins, you might be more partial to passionate bedroom action that evening (always a bonus).
- Creates an obvious opportunity to get dressed up.
- Fosters team work. Remember to be encouraging with lots of smiles and compliments.

Cons:

- Could be frustrating if you, or your partner, lack technique. So keep in mind that you don't need to look like Ginger Rogers and Fred Astaire, you just want to have fun.
- May allow distractions to arise. Remember you're on a Date, so *Keep Your Eyes on the Prize (Your Beloved).* This means you should limit dancing alone, dancing en masse or dancing with others. A brazen rumba with a stranger is best avoided.

- Requires some confidence or lack of inhibition. In La Jolla, California, Himself and I visited the famous La Valencia Hotel for a pre-dinner cocktail. As we were departing, the pianist started to play 'Moon River' which is my favourite song. Himself didn't miss a beat—he whisked me into his arms and waltzed me around their splendid lobby, to the amusement of the hotel's guests. Whilst I'm sure we were not dancing like the stars, I was smiling for the rest of the evening.
- Offers limited talk time, if the romantic aim of your Date is connecting through communication. Endorphins leading you to passionate bedroom action can bypass compassionate conversation—though as listed in the Pros above, this may not be too bad an outcome!

Get Sporty Date – *playful games, outdoor pursuits, physical challenges*

Pros:

- Can spur intimacy when you are physical together; from supporting the other to steady the pool cue, to physically guiding their mini-golf putting or bowling alley technique, to a sensual private dip in a swimming pool.
- Improves teamwork. Sports like mountain climbing and boating require that you help each other and work as a team. Some of us need assistance to ice-skate so end up arm in arm. Lacking coordination, I pretty much need help from Himself on every sport!
- Promotes opportunity for talk time. Sports like fishing, boating, hiking and golf (with its eighteen holes followed by the clubhouse) can provide time for reflection and rich conversation. Himself and I enjoy hikes in the countryside; after a few miles, our dialogue deepens and we begin exchanging new thoughts. Releases endorphins so that your mood is enhanced! Explore racquet sports, skiing, cycling or any other activity that will render you out-of-breath. In a good way.

- Can encompass romantic scenery. Horse-riding, hiking, boating and cycling can include splendid outdoor surroundings. In the UK, rural footpaths are dotted with stiles and small swinging gates, tiny villages and historic pubs, which make a picturesque setting for a romantic Date.

Cons:

- Can raise frustration if either of you become competitive or get bossy. Himself and I lasted all of five minutes on a tandem-bicycle. And sharing a double kayak can involve us going around in circles— each doing our utmost to steer.
- May not be a great Date if the sport is not designed for two. Himself is a yoga nut, and I let that be his thing. Likewise Tai Chi, which also requires an insular focus. Also watch out for team sports. Clearly joining the local volleyball or soccer competition doesn't constitute a Date.
- Might reduce your confidence if you're not competent in the sport.
- Reduces talk time. Playing sports like tennis doesn't naturally involve too much chat. So I suggest incorporating some time when you can take advantage of the endorphins, or enhanced team spirit, and show appreciation for each other.
- Could be a challenge to dress well. Remember it's a Date, so pull out your finest or most flattering sportswear. Grotty old sweats will not do!

Volunteering Date – *shared interest, charity, religious or community event*

Pros:

- Will invariably be a rewarding activity, which could open up interesting conversations about past or future charitable contributions: what's been meaningful? How can you give from your natural strengths? Who are your role models?

- Can encourage good spirits.
- Helping others in need can make you feel grateful for what you have. You might find that you are more appreciative of your spouse or partner.
- May involve the two of you working together as a team.
- Will most likely be inexpensive, unless it's a fund-raising exercise.

Cons:

- Should be more about the charity than about you! By its nature the charity's objectives, and yours for the Date, might not be perfectly aligned.
- May rouse the likeliness that one of you is more passionate about the activity than the other. Simply put, don't sign up for gardening when one of you doesn't like bugs.
- Can involve discomfort and may not endear you to intimacy. If you are clearing refuse from the community park, you might not be feeling too romantically inclined.
- Could be too distracting—many charitable activities can involve large numbers of other people.

At-home Date — *sunset cocktails, picnic in the garden, candle-lit dinner, cards and board games*

Pros:

- Being at home means you can design a Date that is purely about you and your other half—whether it's cooking your partner's favourite meal, playing 'your song' or opening a special bottle of wine brought back from holiday. It's a Date made to order.

- Promotes convenience and comfort. There's less competition for the comfy seat at the bar. And you will have no need to worry about getting home. Or as Himself suggestively asserts—it's just a few steps away from the bedroom.
- Will most likely be inexpensive. Though you may need to spend some money to make the evening special.
- Encourages fewer inhibitions. Out of the public eye, anything goes—well almost. Shy people tend to feel more liberated at home, so if you love to dance but would be embarrassed in public, jiving in your living room might be the answer.
- Lets you play games and have fun. Some games even offer opportunity to be flirtatious. Remember Twister!

Cons:

- Might not be seen as special. After all you are still at home. Psychologists have shown that you are more likely to resort to established 'everyday' behaviours when in 'everyday' surroundings.[29] In which case you will need to create a special scene to signify the otherness of the occasion: you could light candles, buy some new music, put on your party dress and dine in your 'not-everyday' location, such as the proper dining table (if you regularly eat in the television room or at the kitchen counter) or maybe a candlelit porch or balcony.
- Could risk you being consumed by the practicalities of the evening. Activities like preparing food, cleaning up and changing music might take more of your focus than having a romantic time with each other. Neat freaks may be unable to delay loading the dishwasher, in spite of passion calling (but try! Your relationship is

more important than clean dishes). Can be prone to interruptions. The house phone ringing, or the arrival of your teenagers or unannounced friends dropping in.

- Can induce conflict! Amusements like board games and cards can get a little too competitive, even argumentative. Himself and I are always at odds over the correct Scrabble rules. And by the end of the game a sore-loser might be less than loving.
- Playing board games can risk a prolonged diversion from the Intentions of Date Night. If the game requires concentration like Backgammon and Chess, you might find yourselves being insular non-verbal operators, rather than two people primed for romance.

Weekend Date — *city break, rural retreat or spa weekend*

Pros:

- Fosters a sense of romance.
- Gives the opportunity to dress to impress. So be intentional about your packing.
- It's re-energising. Over a relaxing weekend you can catch up on sleep, unwind from your usual stresses, and be recharged for each other.
- Provides plenty of talk time and opportunity, just the two of you, to connect on a deeper level.
- Scores high on convenience. Especially if dining options are provided within the guesthouse or hotel. When we go away I like to dine wherever we are staying, for one of the evenings. This way, there is no need to think about where to go, no need to worry about getting to and from your restaurant, and no need to worry about coats and scarves (a serious consideration when we lived in Ireland).
- Limits interruptions. There are no alarms, no children competing for your attention.

Cons:

- Can be expensive. But it doesn't need to be. Look out for inexpensive but charming guesthouses or Bed & Breakfasts. You could even stay with family and friends (more on how this should work on page 40). We know many people who collect loyalty points with their supermarket, credit cards or air miles, or make much use of Groupon and other online subscriber deals to subsidise their romantic breaks. I also like the idea of paying into a relationship account for your romantic breaks and Dates; they *are* an investment, after all, into the quality of your relationship.
- Requires research and organisation. Appreciating the effort involved can make the weekend even more deservedly special.
- Wears you out, if you organise weekend breaks packed with sightseeing. You might find yourself so busy that you are left too exhausted for romance. Build a relaxing sundowner or 'gin o'clock' into your day's activity.
- Can necessitate overnight childcare. Entrusting your children with family and friends might be your answer for an uninterrupted weekend. Without the distraction of children you are more likely to be relaxed, and have the energy to really focus on each other. If leaving your children is problematic, then you will need to find accommodation that has childcare facilities.

Vacation Date — *beach holiday, cultural exploration, escorted tour, adventure trip*

Pros:

- Supports romance. Most holiday spots have settings or activities that can be simply ideal. For example a cosy cabin in the mountains, a balloon-ride over the countryside, or taking a midnight dip in your private pool or giant 'honeymoon suite' spa bath.

- Limits distractions from your day-to-day life.
- Provides lots of talking time, which actively supports the Manifesto's intimacy-building Intentions.
- Allows plenty of time to gather energy for romance.
- Encourages opportunities to dress to impress. Everyone's talking about 'resort wear'– chic vacation outfits. So 'resort to romance' should be your luggage theme.

Cons:

- May be tiring. Spending an extended time focused on romance might be fatiguing for some. You should agree which days or evenings are Dates and which are more informal and relaxed. It would be a mistake to assume every night is Date Night—unless it is your honeymoon!
- Can be low in 'couple time'. Cruises with group dining, chalet skiing holidays, bus tours and other activity-based holidays can encourage spending more time with a crowd than as a couple.

Surprise Date – *concert tickets, special dinner, new experience*

Pros:

- Receiving a pleasant surprise from someone you love is in itself romantic. The key word here is *pleasant;* for each of us it's something different.
- Helps to energise the Date with a sense of mystery.
- Demonstrates thoughtfulness and attentiveness, due to the effort required to orchestrate a surprise.

Cons:

- Could back-fire as not everyone loves a surprise; some personalities are more receptive to uncertainty than others. Think about how previous surprises have been received. Is your partner genuinely delighted or crying on the inside?
- Be aware—whilst liking a surprise, they may not like *this* surprise. I must admit to sitting on the floor of a hot-air balloon praying for it to land. Vertigo-struck Michelle tells me that just looking up at the Empire State Building makes her feel ill—so her partner's planned trip to the top didn't have the results he was expecting.
- Carefully think through what they might need to fully appreciate the Date, as the surprised spouse might not be dressed or organised to be comfortable for the experience. Do they need spectacles for the theatre? Or a swimsuit for the spa? Himself, who is great at planning romantic surprises, always gives me clues about how to prepare. The occasional clue enjoyably heightens the anticipation of the Date.

Right! Now you have seen my appraisal of Date events, from the lazy movie Date through to the sensual dancing Date. While I predict locking of horns—not lips—on board game or other competitive type Dates, the decadent Weekend Date luxuriating uninterrupted in each other's company is a must for all. And selecting a Date idea that allows you to practise your Date Night Decorum can certainly smooth the path to intimacy and lead to a stronger sense of connection. So take notes, and begin sparking ideas for your next Date today!

Worried that your mate will make an ill-fated Date Night choice? Fear not, even the most unromantic of events can be redeemed—with some effort. (See Principle 2 – Book Your Table for Two.)

Keeping Score

It may seem scary to score your romantic endeavours, but this process will help you to identify those factors which make the romance fizzle or sizzle. On page 201 are all the Principles of the Date Night Manifesto, represented as a score sheet. This keeps track of how you are progressing with your Date Nights. Ideally, you will keep a record of your Date Night performance over a series of Dates, in order to monitor and encourage progress.

After your Date Night, spend thirty minutes reviewing how it worked out. But not on the very same evening (a score card in bed could be misinterpreted), maybe at breakfast the next day, or during the weekend, when you still have a clear memory of the Date. You should briefly discuss and score one Principle at a time. You and your mate have different personality strengths so it's expected that your individual performances will be better on some Principles than others. For example on Principle 9 – *The Etiquette of Flattery,* it may be that your partner gave you plenty of meaningful compliments and you forgot to give a single one—oops!

Award each other between 0 and 5 depending on Principle-related performance.

Starting with the lowest score…

0, 'Oops!' You have ignored this Principle or forgotten you were on a Date Night.

1, Novice. Let's face it, you have been awkward on this Principle. A bit wooden, as if reading from a script.

2, Experienced Beginner. You're able to adjust your approach to the situation. You're freewheeling, but prone to the odd slip-up.

3, Dating Practitioner. You're on the ball, demonstrating skill and flexibility. But missing the finesse for true dating prowess.

4, Smooth Operator. You're good! But not yet the next Romeo. There's still room to grow.

5, The Romantic Maestro. Wow—you compare with the best, Mr Darcy / Ms Mae West. You could be giving *me* lessons.

0 = Oops, 1 = Novice, 2 = Experienced Beginner, 3 = Dating Practitioner, 4 = Smooth Operator, 5 = Maestro

Date Night Score Sheet	Him 0: oops!...5: maestro!	Her 0: oops!...5: maestro!
Date Night Prep		
1. *Get Your Beauty Sleep* – Date when you have energy		
2. *Book Your Table for Two* – agree on a romantic venue		
3. *Find Your Date Night Finery* – dress to impress		
4. *Arrive 'in Smile'* – turn up in good spirits		
5. *Romance Won't Wait (Don't Be Late)* – be punctual		
Date Night Decorum		
6. *Hang off Their Every Word* – behave attentively		
7. *Every Venue Has a Silver Lining* – be positive about the setting		
8. *Toast Your Togetherness* – celebrate your relationship		
9. *The Etiquette of Flattery* – appreciate each other		
10. *Reveal More (but No Strip Tease—Yet)* – share more about yourself		
11. *Wanted: Good Sense of Humour* – foster a lightness of heart		
Date Night Vitamins		
12. *Negativity No-Nos* – avoid negativity		
13. *Be a Lover Not a Fighter* – curtail conflict		
14. *Keep Your Eyes on the Prize (Your Beloved)* – resist distraction		
15. *Take a Break from 'Decisions We Must Make'* – put aside decision making		
16. *Shelve Those Domestic Details* – avoid routine admin		
Total Score		

The aim of the Date Night analysis is that you both continue to learn from the experience, increasing the romance in your relationship whilst enjoying more open communication.

Date Night Total Score

This is just a reference point for you, so that you can see how your Date Nights improve with time. However, it's unrealistic that both of you will score 60 or higher on your first Date Night. If you have scored so high, are you being overly generous? Remember to keep it real.

Date Night Strengths

The three highest scoring Principles are your Date Night strengths; they're probably areas that you're naturally good at. Guard them and be proud.

	Him	Her
1st.		
2nd.		
3rd.		

Date Night Learning Opportunities

By addressing your weakest areas, the three lowest scoring Principles, you have opportunity to make the most noticeable improvement in your Date Night. You can choose to focus on one, or all three, of these at the next Date Night. Remember to revisit the specific Principle chapter for ideas to enhance your dating performance.

	Him	Her
14th.		
15th.		
16th.		

Dealing with
'Date Night Resistance'

Well it looks like *one* of you is reading this book – so we're almost there. Let's say that your other half is not as excited about the Manifesto as you and is even blocking your road to Date Night romance. You're not going to let that stop you, are you? Are you! This chapter details two approaches that you can adopt, depending on your partner's first line of resistance. Which of the following best describes your mate?

Is s/he romantically willing but Date Night resistant?

Naturally romantic, this partner is still resistant to the notion of a 'Date Night'. The Manifesto itself seems an unnecessary challenge, or represents a change that is not immediately appealing. "Why?" this partner might ask.

Is s/he hardly ever romantic and therefore Date Night resistant?

Introducing the Manifesto is likely to yank your reluctant partner out of their comfort zone. You have some work on your hands. Don't worry—read on.

Approach A – for Romantically Willing but Date Night Resistant Partners
There are several things you could try here. You could aim at understanding the source of the resistance, then addressing these concerns. Try negotiating an opportunity to give it a go. This strategy will work best with those who are open to discussion and have been known to change their positions in the face of your logical arguments— or indeed, your persuasive charms.

Alternatively, if you think your romantically inclined partner is simply too stubborn or closed to the idea, try dropping the reference to Date Night. Call it 'just an evening for you and me', 'a special evening for two', 'our time', whatever works for you. Then on this 'special evening' you carry out the Manifesto's Principles yourself. Sneaky huh? More on this later in *The Undercover Date Night* (page 207).

Let's try charming your partner into Date Night first, by appealing to their sense of fun and reinforcing feel-good emotions. Before we get started, here's a sample of what *not* to do. These Date Night introductions wouldn't work even for me! Simply don't:

- Suggest Date Night to your mate while in conversation with others. You'd hardly invite someone on a first Date with other listeners, would you. Doing so may sound flippant and insincere or lead to embarrassment.
- Present it as a threat or in the heat of an argument. For example, "I hate that you have no time for me… I want a Date Night". *I'd* be scared to Date you.

- Raise their defences and patronise your mate by fault-finding. Such as "do you think you can pull yourself away from the TV for a Date with me?"

These next tactics are far more enticing, and more likely to be productive:

- Connect Date Night to an activity that you both enjoy, whether it's theatre or music, exploring new restaurants or going to a sports fixture.
- Call on their sense of play or curiosity – "let's try Date Night for fun and see if we like it".
- Be suggestive – "you might be surprised where we end up…"
- Share your excitement and enthusiasm.

Or appeal to their emotions, with openers like:

- "Let's remember the romance of our first Dates."
- "I would feel really special if you gave it a go."
- "I fear that I've been neglecting you, going on Date Night will help ensure that we have dedicated time for each other."

If your partner still isn't charmed into action, try appealing to their sense of logic. Have a little chat in which you refer to the book's introductory passage *What is Date Night?*, where I covered in more detail the following three common areas of apprehension:

"We're an established couple – why do we need a Date Night?" Because it's one of the most important relationships you will ever choose to have, and preserving anything of value requires energy and investment (page 3).

"Isn't it contrived?" Yes it is, and this actually helps romance to come

about (page 6). The contrived elements associated with a Date Night, reinforce intimacy and focus your effort and energy accordingly.

"How is Date Night different from any other night out?" On a Date Night there's a shared assumption about the romantic intent of the evening (page 6).

Establishing a Date Night is likely to be registered as a *change* in your current relationship pattern. Resistance is commonly recognised as an early stage of change, particularly when it's not of their own making. According to theories on change, helping resistant parties to feel valued, and giving them opportunity to communicate and have input on the nature of the change, can reduce opposition. So don't get uppity about your partner's reluctance—be understanding and get their input. You can encourage them to contribute, by saying:

- "How could the idea of Date Night be more comfortable for you?" Or, "How could I make you feel special on Date Night?"
- "What would you like to do on our Date Night?" The key here is to then make it happen, so that they have a sense of control—so if it's dog racing, I suggest you be gracious and 'go to the dogs'.
- "Timing might not be great for you this week, when might suit you best? After the holiday?" Give them some scheduling options.
- "We can try it for six months and if you still don't like the process, we can stop." Give them a trial period and an opt-out clause—this may ease any apprehension or commitment fear. Some people have a set schedule of weekly activities that they don't want to interrupt. Date Night might also interfere with precious down-time or 'me' time.

Manage the pace of change; introducing a change slowly can make the reluctant dater feel more comfortable.

- Give them a choice on how fast you introduce the Date Night Principles. For example, "We could start with four or five Principles from the Manifesto and add one more each time"; "Choose one or two that are important to you and I'll select one or two".

- Use an established event to introduce the Date Night. In this way it may not be seen as purely 'the Date Night'. For example do you have an anniversary or birthday planned? A special dinner in the diary or theatre tickets already booked? Use this to launch some practise of the Manifesto's Principles.

- Go to a familiar and much loved venue. Then your Date Night will not feel completely foreign. However, I would encourage you to think *special* and not just go to the local neighbourhood burger joint or pub. Himself has a favourite restaurant in London, Le Pont de la Tour at the foot of Tower Bridge, overlooking the River Thames; we went there when we were first dating so it marks a long association with romance.

Now that you have persuaded your cynic into trying a Date Night, read *Putting Your Best Foot Forward* (page 26) to get your Date Nights started. And regardless of why they initially weren't keen, remember to show your gratitude to them for actively participating. "Thanks for trying this out, I really appreciate you doing this for me."

The Undercover Date Night

Someone asked me if, like the book *The Rules* (husband-hunting advice from Ellen Fein and Sherrie Schneider), they could just use the Date Night Manifesto as a checklist for themselves without the need to introduce it to their significant other. The answer is—sure you can! Even if it's merely *you* taking action, initiating a romantic evening and following the Date Night Principles, you will be amazed at the results.[30]

Your spouse or partner will be seduced by your Date Night Decorum: your attentiveness and flattery combined with encouragement and humour.

My friend Alison has shrewdly adopted the *Undercover Date Night*. She is in her sixties, married to Tim for thirty-plus years, and wanted to try Date Night—but Tim scoffed at the idea, thinking it not very manly and a bit 'namsey-pamsey'. Tim is ex-military and not known for easily changing his mind. So Alison let the issue go, and then a week or two later, suggested that they have a special night out because they deserved it. Tim readily agreed. Essentially she was setting up a Date Night and was intent on applying the Date Night Principles. Alison reports that the first evening and subsequent special nights and days out have been enormously successful. Tim's no fool, he realises that Alison is organising Date Nights, but he also likes the fact that she's not calling it Date Night; I suspect he sees it as a sign of Alison's respect and understanding of him. Keep this in mind!

Call it a 'special night out', call it whatever you will—but by agreeing to go on this romantic occasion, your partner will be subscribing to the intimate intent of the evening. You can then personally apply some or all the Principles, such as:

Principle 2 – *Book Your Table for Two* – seeking a suitably romantic venue.
Principle 3 – *Find Your Date Night Finery* – endeavouring to 'dress to impress'.
Principle 6 – *Hang off Their Every Word* – behaving attentively.
Principle 8 – *Toast Your Togetherness* – celebrating your relationship.
Principle 9 – *The Etiquette of Flattery* – giving thanks and compliments.

If you are alert, you can even diffuse your partner's oversights. There's bound to be the odd dating faux pas, given that he or she hasn't read the 16 Principles. For instance, your significant other will not realise the importance of putting aside decision-making and household admin, as addressed in Principles 15 and 16; in these cases you can easily suggest an alternative time for their discussion. On other issues you may find it more of an up-hill struggle. For example, just because *you* are making the supreme effort to be there on time (remember, *Romance Won't Wait* – Principle 5), your partner's famous lack of punctuality might remain untouched. Your determination to *Arrive 'in Smile'* (Principle 4) could fall down when he or she's whinging about their day or journey. Don't fret! Come armed with kind-hearted humour, as detailed in Principle 11, to dispel any angst. Be persistent and enjoy seeing what a dramatic difference *just you* applying the 16 Principles can make.

Approach B – for those with the Date Night Resistant and Rarely Romantic Partner

In some cases, a partner or spouse may simply not be interested in romance—not with you, not with anyone. It's just not in their nature. In this situation, the relationship as it stands probably serves a function the couple are content with. For some, it might serve social standing and financial freedom. For others, it might be the comfortable companionship and ease of domestic arrangements. Those given to philosophy or religion might argue that you have passed through that romantic stage of love to a higher level, or agape love.[31] It's up to you, then, to decide if this state is acceptable to you. For many it might be, but given you're reading this book, it sounds like you actually hope for more. Am I right?

If you have a partner who has sadly lost interest in an intimate connection with you, then you *will* experience Date Night resistance. This may be obvious at the time of the Date Night suggestion, or later while on the Date itself, should they even allow it to go ahead.

June and Spencer recently separated after eleven years of marriage. A year before they parted ways June, eager for a romantic connection, invited Spencer on a Date Night to a special gala dinner at a prestigious hotel in their city. Spencer replied enthusiastically about the dining opportunity, and then invited friends to join. June was dismayed at his inclusion of others, telling me he clearly wasn't getting the Date Night concept. By inviting these companions, Spencer had shielded himself from any intimacy with June.

Where might resistance be coming from? Try carefully exploring; gently ask the 'why' questions. "Why does this make you feel uncomfortable?" "I'm puzzled why you feel this way?" or in June's case: "Why would you invite others on our Date?" You may need to carefully probe three or four times to get to the heart of the issue. If their reluctance is because they simply lack interest in intimacy, how upsetting—especially if you are reading this book to instigate change. Maybe it's time to consider seeking marital or couples counselling. Your partner is still in the relationship after all, so there is hope of a positive outcome.

Could resistance be … Fear?

- Fear that there is something wrong with the relationship. They might see the request for a Date Night as a sign of this. In which case, your reassurance of love and commitment is vital. Communicate your wish to *reinvest* in your romance—surely they will see that this reflects how you value the relationship.
- Fear of going outside their comfort zone—a fear which is most common for the romance-shy. Build confidence by taking it easy, by introducing the Date Night Manifesto Principles slowly (see Approach A, specifically page 204 for more details), and by taking note of the theory below.

- They might be afraid of another big 'F': Failure. Will they let you down on Date Night by not meeting your requirements? Here it's important to play down any expectations and let them know it's about enjoying time together; that even simply time to reconnect would be welcome. Reassure them that Date Night Principles are there to be *practised*—it's not about success or failure. "It's a learning process and together, over time, we'll get better." Make it sound like fun. Because it is!

According to behavioural theorists,[32] a fearful view or negative perception can be broken when one experiences something *positive* from participating in the feared activity. Simply put: a negative mentality which says "I don't like spinach" can be completely turned around with the enjoyable consumption of a mouth-watering Spinach Soufflé. In the Date Night context, this means that if they go on a Date Night, enjoy it and feel special, then high five! It's highly probable that you'll have more Date Nights to come.

So – there are three important elements to success in using this technique:

a) Get them to actually participate, of course!
b) Make sure they *notice* the many positive aspects from the evening.
c) Down-play expectations at the start, to better manage an eventual sense of success.

That's all very well, you may say, but how do I persuade Mr/Ms Reluctance to participate? Answer: you'll have to have to make Date Night feel approachable. For the romance-shy, the Manifesto with its outlined Principles can help here; it's like following a recipe, or set of directions, as opposed to trying to work it out for themselves, or attempting a George Clooney persona. Remember—don't hype up the expectations. The terribly romance-shy may feel better knowing they're aiming at simple things like communication and sharing, or closeness and caring (all sub-facets of romance). Perhaps they find the overarching 'romantic' intent overwhelming, the way that words like 'relationship' and 'commitment' can freak certain folks out! Assure them that you're not expecting passionate fireworks from Date One. You're just wanting to enjoy their company.

How are your negotiation skills? Hopefully you won't need to talk someone down off a ledge or liaise in a hostage situation, but you may need these skills to get Mr/Ms Romance-Shy involved. Try opening with: "What would it take for you to participate in a Date Night? If you take part for me, I could do something special for you. Any ideas? What about a back rub? A foot massage? Some 'you' time?" You may shrewdly find other ways of enticing your other half into participating in Date Night. For example, a friend who often has small wagers with her husband on their Scrabble games used the Date Night as her winning prize. Clever!

OK, let's say you have their agreement to fully participate in the process, and you've also lowered expectations. Now you need to turn plain spinach into that delicious soufflé; focus on making the activity as pleasurable for them as possible. *Putting Your Best Foot Forward* tells you how to get your first Date Night underway. I also recommend that at some point during this Date, you ask them, "What are you enjoying about the evening?" By answering, and having to think about the positives, they may realise that they are actually quite appreciating the occasion. Be casual though. Try not to over-enquire and sound like an anxious evaluator, or their mother.

If you've had a more or less successful Date Night, the final element of this behavioural technique is to *let them know*. No passionate fireworks? Doesn't matter. *Do* confirm that you enjoyed the sense of connection, coupledom or commitment.

Dealing with 'Date Night Resistance' can be a thing of the past, once you pinpoint the real issues. Is it a fear of change, failure or romance itself? Is it a dislike of the Date Night notion? Or an attempt to conserve any spare 'me' time. By adopting a resistance-countering Approach, from A or B, you will soon have your mate agreeing to be your date.

Words of Encouragement

The Date Night Manifesto with its 16 Principles arms you with simple, practical techniques for great Date Nights. It will take you out of your romantic rut. It will focus you on the positive, on each other, having fun and crucially putting aside—if just for a few hours—the distractions of parenting, work, household needs and decision making.

The Date Night Manifesto offers you a framework for resetting your romantic barometer. With a little effort, you will enjoy renewed interest, rekindled romance, re-established closeness and intimacy. You will be saved from the abyss; those silent dinners or dull discussions, that many established couples find themselves mired in.

You can organise your next Date today. *Putting Your Best Foot Forward* shows you how easy it is to get started. If your spouse is holding you back, *Dealing with 'Date Night Resistance'* teaches you how to convert a Date Night-shy spouse into a keen escort.

Observing the Date Night Manifesto can set you up for many years of romance, helping you to enhance the essential elements of your attraction and commitment to each other. You'll be injecting some sparkle back into your usual routine, *and* making a regular investment in the future of your relationship!

Notes

Introduction

1   Powdhavee, N. (2009). Think having children will make you happy? *The Psychologist, 22*(4), 308-310.

Part One: Date Night Prep

2   Vohs, K.D., Finkenauer, C., & Baumeister, R.F. (2011). The sum of friends' and lovers' self-control scores predicts relationship quality. *Social and Personality Psychology Science, 2,* 138-145.

3   Behavioural psychologists, like B.F. Skinner and John Watson, demonstrated though scientific trials how our actions are influenced by environmental feedback. One infamous experiment (and by today's standards ethically dubious) from the 1920s involved Watson conditioning an orphan called Albert B to fear a white rat.

4   Maner, J. K., Gailliot, M. T., Rouby, D. A., & Miller, S. L. (2007). Can't take my eyes off you: Attentional adhesion to mates and rivals. *Journal of Personality and Social Psychology, 93,* 389-401.

5   When engaged in an intimacy-building task (such as Date Night), those experiencing positive affect are relatively more likely to feel closer and more attracted to their partner. Kashdan, T. B., & Roberts, J. E. (2004). Trait and state curiosity in the genesis of

intimacy: Differentiation from related constructs. *Journal of Social and Clinical Psychology, 23,* 792–816.

Part Two: Date Night Decorum

6   Research indicates that 55 – 65% of how a message is received is dictated by non-verbal information. Pease, A. & Pease, B. (2006). *The definitive book of body language.* New York, NY: Bantom Dell.

7   B. F. Skinner. (1965). *Science and human behavior.* New York, NY: The Free Press.

8   West, M. (2012). *Effective teamwork: Practical lessons from organizational research.* Chichester, West Sussex: BPS Blackwell.

9   Bryant, F.B., & Veroff, J. (2006). *Savoring: A new model of positive experience.* Hillsdale, NJ: Lawrence Erlbaum Associates.

10 80% of divorced people say that the marriage broke up because it lost a sense of closeness and they did not feel loved or appreciated anymore. Gigy, L., & Kelly, J.B. (1992). Reasons for divorce: Perspectives of divorcing men and women. *Journal of Divorce and Remarriage, 18,* 169-186.

11 Empirical studies conducted by leading academics, like Dr. Martin Seligman and Prof. Robert Emmon, show a significant correlation between expressing gratitude and psychological well-being (happiness). For more information, read Robert Emmon's (2007) *Thanks!: How practicing gratitude can make you happier* or Martin Seligman's (2002) *Authentic happiness.*

12 Gratitude was found to have predictive power in relationship promotion. Algoe, S., Gable, S.L., & Maisel, N.C. (2010). It's the little things: Everyday gratitude as a booster shot for romantic relationships. *Personal Relationships. 17*(2), 217-233.

13 B. F. Skinner. (1965). *Science and human behavior.* New York, NY: The Free Press.

14 From the Relationship Research Institute, formerly known as the

Family Research Laboratory. This Laboratory was part of University of Washington Department of Psychology and received funding from the National Institute of Mental Health.

15 Professor John Gottman calls this cognitive room your 'Love Map'; the space in the brain where you store information related to your partner. Gottman advocates couples to enhance their Love Maps. For his guidance read *The seven principles for making marriage work* by John Gottman and Nan Silver.

16 Renowned Swiss psychologist Carl Jung considered that human beings instinctively want to 'become heroes or heroines in our own personal dramas'; in other words, we continue to grow and develop to feature in changed circumstances.

17 Officially now the Relationship Research Institute, formerly the Family Research Laboratory at the University of Washington. The research centre promotes the scientific study of relationships and first gained media attention as 'The Love Lab' because of the physiology laboratory; where couples are observed using video, heart rate monitors, and other bio-measures.

Part Three: Date Night Vitamins

18 As referenced by the Hospice Education Institute. This non-profit organisation educates health care professionals on hospice and palliative care.

19 Barsade, S., & Gibson, D. (2007). Why does affect matter in organizations? *Academy of Management Perspectives, 21*, 36-59.

20 A positive mood is proven to increase satisfaction with all kinds of social interactions. Lyubomirsky, S., King, L., & Diener, E. (2005). Benefits of frequent positive affect: Does happiness lead to success? *Psychological Bulletin, 131*(6), 803–855.

21 The ratio of positive interactions to negative in happy couples is 20 to 1, in conflicted couples is 5 to 1, and in soon-to-divorce couples

is 0.8 to 1. John Gottman, Professor Emeritus of Psychology at the University of Washington.

22 You'll also find that positive emotional expression can also catch-on. Barsade S.G. (2002). The ripple effect: Emotional contagion and its influence on group behavior. *Administrative Science Quarterly, 47,* 644-675; Hatfield, E., Cacioppo, J.T., & Rapson, R.L. (1993). Emotional contagion. *Current Directions in Psychological Science, 2, 96-99.*

23 Gottman, J. M. (1994). *What predicts divorce: The relationship between marital processes and marital outcomes.* New York, NY: Lawrence Erlbaum.

24 Willpower is proven to be at its strongest after rest (Baumeister, R.F. (2012). Self control – the moral muscle. *The Psychologist, 25*(2), 112-115.) So remember Principle 1 – *GetYour Beauty Sleep!*

25 Studies explored decision-making over the course of the day as shown in the article by Baumeister, R.F. (2012). Self control – the moral muscle. *The Psychologist, 25*(2), 112-115. Other research focused on factors affecting political conservative attitudes Eidelman, S., Crandal, C.S., Goodman, J.A., & Blancher, J. (2012). Low-effort thought promotes political conservatism. *Personality and Social Psychology Bulletin, 38*(6), 808-820.

26 For more on decision-making and personality read *Introduction to type and decision making* (1997) by Katherine Hirsh and Elizabeth Hirsh.

27 To learn more about courtesan society you might enjoy watching the movie *'Dangerous Beauty'*, starring Catherine McCormack. Set in Venice, this film tells the true story of Veronica Franco, a sixteenth century courtesan.

28 Counselling psychologists and therapists regularly report of significant gains when there is a period of silence.

Date Night Accessories

29 Subconsciously the home could stimulate a pre-set response. This is because we have conditioned ourselves to behaving in a certain way in that environment. The original example of classical conditioning comes from Pavlov's experiments with dogs in the 1920s.

30 In established relationships when one person changes their behaviours, it often acts as a catalyst prompting different responses in the other. Remember also those proven contagion effects: your positive mood can readily catch on.

31 Agape is an altruistic and selfless style of love. It is one of six forms of love that feature in the well-known Love Attitudes Scale (LAS); a questionnaire developed by Clyde Hendrick and Susan Hendrick (1986) and based on the work of sociologist John Lee. Religiously oriented writers from C.S. Lewis to Stephen Kendrick reference agape as a form of love which is both unconditional and voluntary; that you can love your spouse even when he or she is acting unlovable and you can choose to be committed come what may.

32 Such as prominent twentieth century psychologists B.F. Skinner and John Watson. See also note 3.

Giving Credit Where It's Due

The Date Night Manifesto has been a joy to write, largely because of the people who have helped the book come to life. I take my hat off to all those who shared their dating stories with me, as well as the open-minded romantics who tested my Principles on their Dates to ensure that the Date Night Manifesto really worked.

The book provided a treasured opportunity to work intimately with two remarkable friends Joan and Kerry:

Emerita Professor of Psychology, Joan Woodworth, who believed in me and saw the potential for the book. Together we validated the premises that underpin the Principles. Joan also gave me the courage to circulate the first draft and to delete thousands of words of carefully crafted text.

Kerry Lander, radio creative and word-wizard, who helped me to release the manuscript from its previously prim textbook tone and to embrace a sassier, easy-listening voice for your reading pleasure. Kerry is also my grammar guru: through her I've learnt the virtue of the approachable em-dash versus the more rigid parenthesis.

Last but not least, Himself, who is credited with being the most gracious mate, indulging my dating explorations and generously allowing our Dates to be shared with you.

More about Myself

I am a romantic, and a psychologist. Both are equal qualifications, I feel, for the researching and writing of this book, which aims to help myself, my friends, *all* of us to enrich our relationships.

I love to get glammed up; my closet is bursting with evening dresses. I like to cook and host intimate dinner parties where I cherish thought-provoking yet fun conversation. Yes, astute onlookers might note my application of some Date Night Principles here!

In spite of being quite shy, which some people consider 'aloof', I like to observe people, make their acquaintance and discover what makes them tick.

You can find me typing in our local cafe with a Grande Americano (hot milk on the side). Here I'm most certainly *not* dressed up, being often garbed in my early morning pilates clothes.

At the time of writing Himself and I have been together sixteen years. We first started dating when he invited me to join him for tango classes—he was good, I was a clumsy mess. After several years together in London (and lots of dance lessons), we moved to Ireland and now live in Dubai, in the Middle East, where we continue to savour our Date Nights.

More about Himself

In some respects Himself is my opposite. Opposites attract, they say. He is cheeky, charming, and enjoys the buzz of a crowd. In a single weekend, he's been known to attend an opera, an Elton John performance and Formula Drift racing!

In other ways we are similar. Himself likes to dress well. He prizes his great grandfather's suit (even though it's too small to wear). Himself shops in Jermyn Street, home to London's finest men's tailors for more than 300 years. His other shopping indulgence is second-hand bookshops, where he'll lose track of time as he slowly takes in each and every shelf.

I adore his manners. In his opening of doors and carrying of my bags, he is a true gentleman. Romantic too—he seeks out those Agatha Christie/colonial-era hotels for our weekends away.

Finally, I admire his discipline. Himself is dedicated to his Ashtanga yoga, which he practises daily at dawn. The same commitment (and flexibility) can be seen in his willingness to participate and learn from our Date Nights. For that, I'm forever grateful.

If you would like more information on this book, Date Nights and romance in general visit www.datenightmanifesto.com.